JUMP SHOOTING

THE GREAT MARSH

*Stories and Lessons from a
Lifetime of Waterfowl Hunting*

JOE GRAY

ISBN: 979-8-9940082-0-1

10 9 8 7 6 5 4 3 2 1

Published by: Marcus Marsh Press
Written by: Joe Gray
Cover design by: Peter Selgin
Proof reading by: Louise D. Stahl
Internal design / typesetting by: Brad Graham

Dedicated to all of the people
who love the outdoors, hunting
and conservation.

DISCLAIMER

This book is a true account of my experiences in the Great Marsh and surrounding areas. Some names and identifying details have been changed to protect the privacy of the individuals involved. Certain events have been condensed, combined, or reconstructed from memory. Any resemblance to persons, living or dead, beyond those intentionally portrayed, is coincidental.

The thoughts, interpretations, and recollections expressed here are my own.

Joe holding a Black duck.

ABOUT THE AUTHOR

A LOT OF HUNTERS WILL TALK ABOUT A ONCE-in-a-lifetime bird dog. How they'll be your best friend while also making you a better hunter, tracker, outdoorsman, and conservationist. How they'll make you more patient, disciplined, calculated, and aware. They'll help you meet people you otherwise wouldn't and help build on the relationships you already have. Put simply, they'll change your life. And once you've hunted with one, hunting without one loses its appeal. Based on that description, Joe Gray could be mistaken for my once-in-a-lifetime bird dog ... which is only reinforced by the number of birds I've shot that he's run down through waist-deep marsh mud, half-frozen creeks, or briars thicker than frozen peanut butter. However, a dog might make for more of a conversationalist. Joe and I share a unique passion, energy and style that facilitate entire conversations and hunts without uttering a single word. This makes communication on the marsh simple, while simultaneously perplexing our wives. "How's Chelsea?" my wife will ask upon my return from a hunt. "I dunno." "How's their bedroom renovation going?" "No idea." "Well, how did the magazine shoot go?" "Not a fuckin clue," I'll answer. "Weren't you guys just together for the last six hours?" "Yup." "Well, do you have any updates from them?" "I know Joe has a new 20 gauge that he folded a bufflehead with at fifty yards." I only wish I could communicate with everyone else the same way. Joe never has to ask me if I have time or motivation to jump just one more creek—it's wasted breath because the answer is always the same: "Let's go for two." One of my biggest fears in life is the day Joe doesn't ask not because he assumes we're going, but because he knows I can't ...

When that day does come, I know my best friend will adapt to the times and shift gears to sitting around a fire down at my gazebo by the marsh, telling hunting stories of old.

Or maybe we'll just sit in silence ... for old times' sake.

Undoubtedly, we'll retell our greatest hunting story— the day we met. A story that I told at the beginning of Joe's wedding ceremony, where he honored me with the task of officiating. He returned the favor telling the story at my wedding as my best man ...

It was a rainy spring Sunday in MA as I wandered the hunting aisle at Dick's Sporting Goods. I was perusing through adult face paint and doe urine when a strong voice with the subtlest hint of nervousness from over my shoulder asked, "Do you, ah, come here often?" I turned around and the trajectory of my life changed forever. I hadn't been raised a hunter. No one in my family hunted. I was introduced to it through a friend and fumbled around the woods for a couple years until I met Joe. He took me under his wing and showed me the world, and by world, I mean the marsh. Flash forward ten years and I am a volunteer International Hunter Education Association instructor, DU chapter chairman, mentor for the youth waterfowl and pheasant hunts, and spend every minute and penny I have on the pursuit of game. I even went so far as to buy a house directly on the marsh. And Joe is no longer the random guy I met at Dick's.

He's loyal to a fault, a dedicated friend to so many, and has a bird drive like nothing I've ever seen, but Joe's no dog. He's a model citizen, ambassador of conservation, loving son, brother, and husband, and my once-in-a-lifetime hunting buddy.

—*Kagan Longval*

Contents

The Definition of Jump Shooting

A type of waterfowl hunting that anyone with any skill can participate in. This style of hunting is referred to as "Jump Shooting" due to the element of surprise when approaching an area where ducks and geese will be. If done correctly, while walking through creeks and jumping over them, you can sneak up on waterfowl close enough to take a shot. Jump Shooting is best for hunters with zero patience.

1

INTRODUCTION
TO HUNTING

IT TOOK ME YEARS OF HUNTING AS A TEENAGER and young adult to really figure it out. In the beginning I just wanted to kill shit. It was a natural instinct for my brother and I to kill fish and birds. It took about fifteen years of hunting to really figure out why I love it so much. When I got out of the Navy, I started to really focus on waterfowl hunting. I didn't hunt much while I was in the service, and I missed it. I wasn't sure what I wanted to do with my life when I entered back into the civilian life, but I knew hunting and fishing would always be there for me. I knew I wanted to dedicate my life to the outdoors professionally. I got my 100-Ton Near Coastal Captain's License to try to start a fishing charter business, but that wasn't it. I volunteered my time as an Angler Education Instructor for the state of Massachusetts, but that wasn't doing it. Worked as a stern man on a commercial lobster boat for a few months, that wasn't doing the trick either. I dug deep into my duck hunting memories and remembered the time my dad and I were checked by the local game warden off Stackyard Road in Rowley. I remember thinking to myself, "Wow, that would be the best job in the world!" So, that's what I dedicated my late twenties to, becoming a Conservation Law Enforcement Officer. I got an associate degree in environmental science, worked part-time as an assistant harbormaster in Manchester by the Sea. I taught Hunter Education classes as a volunteer, and eventually created a kids education program to teach kids about the ocean and its surroundings. I eventually did get hired as an EPO, but that's not what this book is about. So, now that you know I may have some experience with duck hunting in the coastal northeast area of Massachusetts, let me share with you what I have learned over the last twenty years.

My grandfather's name was Warren Alfred Gray, born and raised in Beverly Farms in the 1920s. He once took the train into Boston to buy his first .22 from Sears when he was sixteen. He was raised as an only child and his father taught him how to hunt and fish. He supplemented most of those skills by being self-taught. He was primarily a bird hunter, local waterfowl and pheasants. He would occasionally take a trip to upstate NY for a turkey hunt with his two sons, one of whom was my father. Hunting and fishing were a way of life for most men growing up in the 1930s and '40s. I have the majority of my grandfather's hunting and fishing licenses that he purchased throughout his life, starting in 1939 when he was seventeen years old. He was awarded a free hunting license when he served in the Navy during World War II between the years of 1943 and 1946. Warren Gray was a true American outdoorsman / ball buster who taught his sons how to fish and hunt.

Uncle Rob, Uncle Dick, Gramp Gray, and Grammy Gray in front of the famous deck.

Some of the earliest memories I have are listening to hunting and fishing stories told by my grandfather and father. Now in my thirties, I have heard these same stories hundreds of times and yet I still appreciate them as if it was the first time hearing them. My dad also grew up in Beverly Farms. He was more of a troublemaker than his father, not a criminal, but enjoyed having fun and pushing some limits, like fishing 100 lobster traps with ten different ten-trap licenses. At that time, there was nothing saying you couldn't do it. My father taught my brother and me how to fish and hunt at a very young age. We didn't know how to do much else. Only being on this planet a few years, my brother and I had a passion we were born with, to catch and kill shit. We were taught the basics on how to catch freshwater fish; we would bike around town with fishing rods and pull fish from every single body of water we could ride our bikes to. In the springtime, my dad would bring us to Moosehead Lake in Rockwood, Maine with my grandfather and fish for brook trout and salmon. During the summers we would travel out to Idaho and Montana and catch Clark Fork River Cutthroats. We would wake up when the sun came up and wouldn't stop fishing until the stars came out, every day, for seven days straight. When we weren't fishing out west, we were home catching stripers, either from shore or on Dad's boat on the weekends. When I was little, my dad taught us to always check out the streams running under bridges to see if they looked like a good fishing spot. To this day I cannot physically not look at a body of water when I drive over it.

When I was around ten years old, lobstering was introduced into the mix, and when my brother was twelve, he bought his first boat, known as "The Red Boat." This boat gave us a platform for killing shit for nearly twenty years. At around the age of eight is when I got the passion for waterfowl hunting. I would go with my dad and brother every chance I got. My brother got his first shotgun at age ten, a single shot 20-gauge Ducks Unlimited Green Wing shotgun. I remember exactly when he got it, at his birthday party at Tucks Point in August in a public park. The rest of the presents he got were basketballs, frisbees, toys, and other things ten-year-olds would get each other. That following duck season I remember hunting at The Old Mill and watching my brother reach out and poke at a Black Duck with that gun and dropping it dead on the train tracks. My brother, being almost three years older than me, got most of the shooting in as I watched. When I turned twelve it was game time! My brother was almost fifteen and was distracted by other things. I would go hunting every Saturday morning with my dad. He would bring his 16-gauge L. C. Smith double-barrel and we would go jump shoot ducks off of Town Farm Road in Ipswich at low tide with the dogs. I started hunting before I legally could, but my dad was always there and would make sure we were safe. He also let us shoot at everything, he would always say "It's not going to fall if you don't shoot!" Later in life I have mastered a fifty-plus yard shot at a duck flying fifty mph giving it a four-foot lead and still being able to drop it dead, but we'll get to that later.

My mom always supported whatever type of animal or bird we brought home. She would turn it into pot pie or a delicious baked dish. My entire life I would come home smelling like fish or covered in mud, and I knew the severity of it when she was waiting at the door to tell me to strip down to my boxers on the back deck before I attempted to enter the house. That was pretty much her only rule. My mom grew up on the west coast, joined the United State Coast Guard and traveled around different areas of the world, like Hawaii, and was on an Ice Breaker in Alaska before she ended up in Boston where she met my dad. She spent twenty years in the Coast Guard as a Chief Radioman. If you were to meet her now, you would never guess that she had done all of that before having two boys that would give her so much stress and anxiety. She never liked the ocean very much; she always hated not being able to see the bottom of the ocean. But she still went fishing with us almost every time; until we started getting older and much bolder with our fishing techniques. Any time we would bring home a fish, she knew exactly what to do with it. We knew that we needed to clean and skin the striper before bringing it home. She makes the best baked Striped Bass;

she always cooked it in the same white oval baking dish, topped with crumbled Ritz crackers, butter, and fresh cut lemon on the side. But her best and most famous recipe is her deep-fried lobster. It's a ton of work, but I have never had lobster served a better way. From the ages of twelve to seventeen, my brother and I would bring home a few lobsters almost every day after lobstering. Eventually she developed a one-of-a-kind recipe for deep frying them. She has tried dozens of different batters and only one made the cut, New England Batter, and we could only find it at Market Basket. She would also use vegetable shortening in the deep fryer for the oil. I'll add the recipe toward the end of the book for you all to enjoy. I don't know if my mom ever willfully killed a fish or bird on her own, but she gave us nothing but support and love regardless of how disgusting we were when we came home from a fishing or hunting adventure.

My brother has this passion for being a professional at hunting and fishing. Some people say that there is no way that he can kill two, eight-point deer and five does in a single season without doing it illegally. But he takes an enormous amount of pride in doing everything lawfully. It is far more satisfying doing it the right way, unless you are some sick criminal that enjoys the thrill of trying to get away with it. Those people are known as poachers, and he is far from one. He has this unique drive that other people are not born with. So, it is hard for them to relate and try to figure out how he is so good at hunting and fishing. The only way that I can describe how good he is, is to just watch him. There is something about his fishing and hunting charisma.

My wife is a lover of all living things, except mice and rats. She hates when I trap and kill them though. I used to live trap city rats at our old apartment and release them in nearby affluent towns so they could live a better life, just because she did not want me to kill them. She had always told herself that she would never marry a "hunter." She can barely kill a fly without feeling bad for it. She doesn't understand how I can shoot a duck when hunting but save animals when not hunting. I believe it is something that she will never understand, but what she does understand is how much passion I have for waterfowl hunting and how much it means to me. She may not support hunting, but she supports me.

2

THE GREAT MARSH

THE MARSH HAD SUCH A GREAT POPULATION OF waterfowl that it was once recorded that one gentleman killed sixty Canada Geese during a winter storm only using a club as a weapon. Most of my hunting experience is on The Great Marsh. This marsh covers nearly 20,000 acres of waterfowl habitat spanning from Salisbury to Gloucester. All this marsh is open to waterfowl hunters, except the Parker River National Wildlife Refuge. The smart birds winter on the refuge; if you ever get a chance to go visit, bring some binoculars. There are always a few pairs of beautiful drake Pintails hanging out fifty feet from the road. Although it is the same marsh, these birds know which side of the river is safe. I always hear rumors that at least two pairs of Pintails are taken every year on the Northern portion of the Great Marsh, but

I have never personally seen a drake Pintail harvested. Here in Massachusetts, there is a common phrase known as "The Right to Fowl, Fish, and Navigate." This is the ancient and colonial ordinance of 1641. It essentially says that you (the hunter) have the right to fowl (lawfully waterfowl hunt / bird watch), fish (lawfully engage in fishing), or navigate tidal property where the tide ebbs and flows. What all of that means is that you can lawfully waterfowl hunt on all tidal property (property affected by the tide) regardless if the property is public or private. You just cannot cut through private property to access the tidal property. Most of the 20,000 acres of marsh is privately owned, but due to the "Fowl, Fish, and Navigate" law, you can lawfully waterfowl hunt there. Hunters have been hunting the Great Marsh for hundreds of years.

3

SHOTGUNS

YOU ARE GOING TO WANT A SHOTGUN THAT IS reliable and can take a lot of abuse. The salt marsh is no friend of a shotgun, just one time that gun is not cleaned before being put away, it is almost guaranteed that there will be rust somewhere on it the next time you go to grab it. I shot a Benelli Nova 12-gauge pump for years. That gun has taken some serious abuse. I have fully submerged it in saltwater, drained it, made sure the barrel was clear of any obstructions, and successfully fired a round through it. After many rounds fired through that gun, the trigger guard pins tend to back out. Another time, I was jump shooting behind Sudbay's in Gloucester, jumped a Black Duck out of the creek, shot it, racked the pump to the rear, and the trigger guard and bolt assembly fell out and landed on the muddy marsh. I didn't want my hunt to be over, so I re-assembled it and tried to chamber a round. Not feeling very safe, I walked back to my truck, put two Zip Ties through the trigger pin holes, tightened it the best I could and continued the hunt. I kept using the shotgun in that stage until I received the new pins in the mail. I would normally only do a deep clean on that gun once a year. After every hunt I would spray some Rem Oil on the metal parts and put it away. During one blizzard a few years back, I was hunting with my dad and a now late friend, Bart Waldo. We were hunting in weather that was so miserable, every few minutes we questioned why we were there in the first place. We each had our own gun. I had my Nova, Bart had a Browning A5, and my dad had a Remington over-under. The temperature that day was in the single digits and visibility was about thirty feet. The wind was so strong that ducks could barely fly, which caused them to fly very low looking for cover. This made for some excellent shooting. Well, it would have if both mine and my dad's firing pins didn't freeze in place. We eventually just passed around the A5 and each took turns at shooting as birds flew over to check out our decoys. That was the last time I was honored to hunt with Bart before his passing. Once I returned home and warmed up enough to feel my hands again, I took apart my Nova to see what the issue was. She was so dirty that there were enough dirt particles and old grease to freeze that firing pin in place with the extreme low temperatures. Now I do a full clean on the Nova twice a year.

TYPES OF SHOTGUNS

MY GRANDFATHER ALWAYS HAD A GUN CABINET in the basement that was off limits, so, of course, we got into it. There were a few old Damascus side-by-sides. My dad found out firsthand that Damascus barrels cannot support new shells. But on the wall to the left of the cabinet were a few .410 shotguns, one single-shot, and one bolt-action. I always wanted to shoot them. When my grandfather was on his way out, I asked him if I could have them. He gave me every gun that was left in the house. He was a personal fan of the Ithaca Featherweight 12-gauge pump. The .410 caliber shotgun is mainly used for small game and clay shooting. I hope someday I can kill a goose with that single-shot. I wouldn't recommend this size gun for jump shooting ducks and geese. It will technically work, but it's just not the most productive and ammo is tough to find for it.

I first heard about the 28 gauge from an upland hunting game I had on my family computer when I was eight or nine. I have never shot one, nor have I really seen one out on the marsh. They are commonly used for breaking clays and upland bird shooting. The ones I have seen usually bring a four-figure price, not something that you would want to expose to saltwater and mud. But I would, if I had one. What good is a fancy gun if it's not being used?

This past season I bought a Stevens 320 20-gauge

15

pump-shotgun for $150, brand new. The reason I purchased this exact gun is because I wanted a challenge to try to shoot waterfowl with the cheapest shotgun around. I picked up this gun from the gun shop, brought it home and immediately opened the box like a little kid on Christmas. I inspected the gun to see how poorly made it was and was not very disappointed. I bought two different chokes, Carlson's Mid-range and Full. I threw on a custom leather sling and took it on the marsh. I wasn't quite sure what to expect bringing a 20 gauge on the marsh. I snuck up on a creek that almost always has birds in it and flushed about thirty Black Ducks. I fired three shots at three different ducks, and nothing fell. I was very disappointed at first thinking that this gun was shit and the rest of my jump shoot was ruined for the day. I reloaded another three shells and watched a pair of Black Ducks circle back around and fly about thirty-five yards away from me. I raised my gun, put a two-foot lead on the bird, and pulled the trigger. One of the two ducks folded up and hit the ground stone dead. I was shocked. Mark retrieved this bird, and my hope was restored that my hunt wasn't over. I then jumped another duck at about fifteen yards and took one shot, dropping it to the ground. I was starting to really like this gun. I continued to hunt the entire season with this gun, and I now put this shitty 20-gauge pump in my top three favorite shotguns to hunt waterfowl with. I made great shots at fifty yards, shot geese with it, and hit birds at fifteen feet. This gun was so much fun to use, I highly recommend trying it out.

Marcus proudly lying next to a limit of Black Ducks taken with a 20-gauge pump.

MY DAD'S 16 GAUGE IS THE GUN MY BROTHER AND I are going to fight over when it's that time. But for now, I have it. Each gun has a story. I understand to some people a gun may appear as some metal and wood, and as a dangerous assault weapon to the majority of human beings. But if you are reading this book, you and I both know that each gun has its own personality. Most guns commonly identify as female. She prefers a certain type of ammo; she has good days and bad. If you miss a bird it's most likely your fault, if she misfires, probably your fault too. You didn't keep her clean or tried to cycle rusty ammo through her. At the end of the day, regardless of what you used her for, she gets oil rubbed all over her, shoulder mounted as if you were in the field, and put away loved. If you take care of her, she will take care of you for the rest of your life. When my dad was in the Coast Guard in 1978, he had sent some money home to his father to buy him a shotgun for when he got home from Iwo Jima. I think it was around $300 and my grandfather picked up a L. C. Smith 16-gauge side-by-side for when he returned. This gun has been part of my life since I was five years old. My dad would always wipe her down with Hoppes oil and we would watch. To this day when I smell Hoppes I immediately think about that gun and watching my dad and grandfather clean their shotguns after hunting. I shot my first bird with this gun. This year I brough her out for a jump shoot with my new pup Marcus. I had a single Black Duck come in from the right heading left. I lined it up with the massively wide aiming platform a side-by-side has to offer, gave it a twelve-inch lead and pulled the trigger. At twenty yards the bird fell dead, Marcus retrieved the bird and brought it back to me. I knew she (the gun) loved the attention.

Mark showing his roots sitting next to a Black Duck and my dad's 16 gauge.

WHEN I WAS FOURTEEN YEARS OLD, MY DAD GOT me my first shotgun for Christmas. This gun was a Remington 870 Magnum with a raised rib. My dad always spoke highly of the raised rib; he never had one but one of his friends did and was always told that it was a good thing to have one. So, now I have my own. This specific 870 did not have a traditional blued finish, it had more of a flat finish which was great on the marsh because it didn't shine when the sun hit it. The only bad part about the barrel was that it held salt really well, and salt on a metal barrel is recipe for disaster if you do not clean that gun immediately when you get home. The finish would begin to form rust within twenty-four hours if not wiped down after only a few hours on the marsh. Even at seventeen years old when I started hunting on my own and sometimes my dad was not home when I got back, I still wiped down that gun right when I got home and put it in the gun closet. I also highly recommend to never store your gun inside a soft or hard case. The foam padding inside the case can hold water and moisture. If you leave your gun in its case, I can almost guarantee the next time you take your gun out it will be covered in rust. I learned that the hard way with my 870, of course, that one time I didn't listen to my dad. I got home from hunting one Saturday evening, tossed my gun in its case into the gun closet, and didn't break it back out until the following Saturday before heading out to the marsh. I pulled the gun out of the case and was devastated by the rust damage. It was mostly surface rust but there was some deep pitting on some parts after I cleaned it. ALWAYS wipe down your gun after hunting on the marsh.

At around eighteen years old, I wanted to upgrade my marsh gun so that this would never happen again. I went up to Kittery Trading Post and bought myself a Benelli Super Nova 12-Gauge Pump. I was the first person in my family to ever purchase a gun with a synthetic stock and wrapped barrel. This gun had Max-5 marsh print, interchangeable chokes, and could take 3.5" shells. I put a sling on it and hunted the hell out of it. I had that gun for only three or four years until it got stolen when I was living in Virginia while I was in the Navy. Everything worth value in my house was stolen, the loss of that gun is the only thing that to this day still hurts. I didn't have much time to hunt in the Navy, just when I returned home during the season, which was once or twice over a four-year span. That was one of my biggest regrets during the time I served; I never hunted and barely fished while I served. Although I did travel halfway around the world via nuclear powered submarine and slept next to my L.L.Bean 8 wt fly rod. I had good intentions to use it at every port, but by the time we pulled in we all just went straight to the bars. I did get to make a few casts off the back of the boat while we were in Crete, Greece. I wish someone had gotten a picture of me double hauling on the stern of a US submarine with Crete's beautiful mountains and the Mediterranean Sea in the background. I'll let you imagine how amazing that was for me. I think I only caught a few small pier fish, but that didn't matter. February 12th, 2014, I returned home from the Navy for the final time. The following morning I broke out my old rusty 870, grabbed my dad's hunting dog Stella, and we went for a nice long walk on the marsh. It was late goose season, so the odds of actually shooting a passing goose on the marsh were pretty low, but I was home, in my favorite place in the world, with my dog and gun.

During the 2022 waterfowl season I acquired two different 10-gauge shotguns, my dad's single shot and my father's life-long hunting partner and best friend Ithaca Mag 10. This Mag 10 is such a special gun. I've heard countless stories about it my entire life. This gun belonged to Kevin Kelleher, a name that was associated with every hunting story I've ever heard from my father. A few days before the last day of early goose season I reached out to Kevin and asked if he still had this legendary 10 gauge. He said yes and told me to come get it. When I arrived at his house, I walked through his back door into his kitchen and saw this incredible shotgun, looking like it had never been used. I picked it up, all fifty-three inches and twelve pounds of it, and drifted off for a second, imagining what damage this thing would bring to the goose population in the North Shore. When I came back to reality, Kevin told me that it never cycled shells and would jam constantly. He said he never killed anything with it and there had never even been an entire box of shells put through her. He bought the gun from a gun shop in Newbury in the early '80s. I brought the gun home along with two 1950s Remington 870's that Kevin told me to hang on to until he wants them back. When I took her home, I called James and told him that I was gifted with an Ithaca Mag 10 cannon. Somehow, he bought a 10 gauge and two boxes of shells within a three-day period of when I got mine. On the last day of early goose season 2022, James, Ringo, Robby, and I hit Bartletts Farm for the last two hours of shooting hours. It was the best goose hunting I have ever had. After the first round of birds dropped stone-cold dead by my new Mag 10, I sent Kevin a picture and told him she is working flawlessly. These 10 gauges hit so damn hard that we did not have a single crippled goose on the ground. But the birds just kept coming after we ran out of 10-gauge ammo. Luckily, I brought my trusty Nova and three boxes of 12-gauge shells for her. We shot forty-one birds in a sixty-minute window. Out of those forty-one birds, we unleashed at least fifty rounds of 10 gauge and another seventy-five rounds of 12-gauge shells. A few days later we heard from the farmer that they were concerned about how many shots we let rip. Now, you never want to piss off the landowner because they can kick you off the property whenever they want. So, we decided to help them out prior to this year's early goose season and rebuild 100 yards of road for them to essentially apologize for all the shooting. We now restrict the gauge size to Bartletts, so it doesn't happen again.

Early goose season damage with 10 gauges.

OH, THE BIG BEAUTIFUL 10 GAUGE, WHAT AN excellent shotgun. These guns are very special to me. My dad always spoke very highly of his single shot H&R 10 gauge. I've never tried it, but he claims it's a seventy-yard gun. I've only fired it twice and I don't doubt it. Out of those two times one of them was a one-on-one, goose vs. hunter challenge. It was the last day of late season and James and I went for a 10 gauge, late season, free for all, jump shooting adventure on the marsh. We took his boat in from the launch behind Marky's. While transiting toward the back of the marsh where the geese roost, we put up nearly 100 Black Ducks, as always, duck season was closed for the year. He dropped me off in a half-filled creek within sixty yards of a salt panne that had over 300 geese in it. I had both of my 10 gauges with me, the single and the semi. James drove his boat another 200 yards down the creek where he anchored, and it wasn't long before he jump shot three geese. Now that the world knew we were jump shooting with 10 gauges, the geese were everywhere by the thousands. James shot two more geese during the frenzy. I took some far shots with the Mag 10, but nothing successful. The scene calmed down as the shooting stopped and the geese flew very far away. I then heard a single honk; I looked in the direction of the honk and saw one lonely goose looking for his friends. I let a few honks out and got its attention. This bird flew directly toward me from almost a mile away. Now with it approaching, I had one of two options; a single shot gun for a single goose, or increase my odds of putting it on the ground with three shots from the Mag-10. I picked up the single shot to be fair. This single goose was now closing inside of thirty yards. I knew I only had one shot, one opportunity to drop this bird. As I popped up from the creek, the bird flared away from me, I cocked back the hammer, gave the bird a ten-inch lead and pulled the trigger. That bird folded so hard, by the time it hit the ground it was lights out, dead. This shot was one of my favorites because I did everything perfect and put that bird on the ground, there were no mistakes made.

I recently had the opportunity to purchase an absolute unit of a 10 gauge; this is a side-by-side, thirty-two-inch double barrel, fixed full chokes, double trigger, beautiful gun. She was made sometime in the 1960s–70s and there is surprisingly not much info about her on the internet. She was made by Mercury and / or Tradewinds, model 1032. That is all I know about it; oh yeah, she might be Spanish, but because of her age it is frowned upon to shoot modern steel shot through her fixed full-choke barrels. Ten-gauge ammo is very expensive and hard to find, so, after hours of contemplation, I pulled the trigger and purchased 100 rounds of Boss Copper plated Bismuth, 3.5" #1 2 1/8 oz shells. Now at $3.35 a round, I highly wouldn't recommend using the gun during early goose season when you can shoot fifteen birds a day. She's a classy gal and will get the job done, but expensive to take out like most girls, I mean guns.

Jump shooting with a half dozen goose silhouettes, a side by side 10 gauge, and a solo layout blind.

FALL OF 2014, I STARTED TO HIT THE MARSHES, ponds, and fields hard. I was getting back the passion I once had before I joined the Navy. Now I was older, a little bit smarter, and had the patience I needed to become a better hunter. One specific day while hunting Magnolia Fields in Gloucester, I was having a bad day of hunting. Everyone around me was using a Benelli Super Black Eagle II. They were dropping birds left and right and with my 870, I felt like I was just scaring them or crippling the birds at best. I ended up crippling three geese and my brother two. These crippled birds landed in the pond behind us. Being the younger brother, it wasn't even a negotiation, it was my job to go get them. I got into a solo canoe, and I had five shells left. I paddled up to the three birds, placed a good headshot on each of them, and picked them up. The fourth bird I had to use two shots on it to be able to retrieve it. Now I have zero shells, and one bird left to retrieve. This bird had a busted wing so it wasn't very mobile, I thought if I paddled close enough to it, I could just grab it. As I approached this bird, about three feet away, it dove under water. I never knew that geese could dive, but sure enough, they can! I watched the bubble trail to try to predict where it was going to pop up. I approached this bird to attempt to grab it and it just dove again. So, my next thought was maybe if I get within the length of the paddle away from it, I can use the paddle as a tomahawk and smash it over the head. I attempted this method about three or four times. On the fifth swing I made perfect timing and contact. My brother, Bob, and Jay were on the shore laughing so hard I could hear them from 150 yards away. I got the five birds with five shells and five swings of the paddle. After returning to shore with the slight feeling of success but mostly defeat, the following day I went and bought myself a new Benelli Nova 12 gauge. I have always preferred a pump over a semi-auto, mostly because I could never afford one, but there's nothing like a pump shotgun, the sound of the pump action is one of the most iconic sounds on this planet. When you hear that sound, you better be the one making it and not on the other side of it. I now have been hunting with a pump for over twenty years, semi-autos may be nice, but I can easily outshoot someone with an auto with my Nova. A pump action shotgun to me is like a wrench to a mechanic. I always describe to people that my Nova is a tool that I use while hunting, I don't see it as a gun.

At some point over the next few years, I purchased myself a Stevens 555 12-gauge over-under. I primarily bought it for shooting pheasants at Kents Island in Newbury. This gun has a perfect balance for me, and the light weight makes it very easy to carry all day. I love the way it comes up and swings left to right. After shooting a few pheasants with it, I wanted to use it more, so I started to bring it duck hunting in flooded timber ponds and swamps. This gun was perfect for this type of shooting. I refer to this style as "Woods Ball," kind of like "Street Hockey" or "Street Ball." I don't think anyone else calls it that, but that's what I call it when I hunt flooded timber. With an improved choke on top and modified on bottom, this was a perfect tool for shooting woodies, teals, and mallards as they cut and weave through the trees. Some people have questioned me when I pull out an over under to go bang ducks in the swamp. What's the point of having a shotgun if you don't plan to use it. That gun does not appreciate sitting in a dark gun safe year after year waiting to go hunting, bring her out and let her have some fun! This year I only used my 555 for duck hunting; I wanted to make better shots for training Mark, and it made me a better shooter. Knowing that I only had two shots instead of three and that I did not have an extra full choke like in the Nova, I knew I had to focus more and get closer to birds to drop them dead for Mark to retrieve them. For most of my hunting life, every day I went hunting I would bring no less than twenty-five shells with me. The reason for this was because I would take ridiculously far shots and I never wanted to run out. This year I would bring six-eight shells with me. You can legally shoot six ducks and two geese during the normal season. That has pretty much never happened, but that's where my mind was at, one shot per bird. The amount of focus and discipline I had this year was like no other. This year I wouldn't even shoulder my gun unless I knew for a fact that I could drop that bird, so that's what I did. I only shot about sixteen–eighteen ducks this year, but I shot less than a box of shells. I did kill approximately forty geese during the early season, I'm glad I got that out of the way before the duck season started.

Woods Ball; a muddy over under and a pair of Mallards.

4

ESSENTIAL EQUIPMENT AND GEAR

CHOKES

Choke tubes are very important depending on the style of hunting you plan on doing. There are three types of chokes you should consider while jump shooting the marsh. Modified, Full, and Extra-Full. Well, that's how I did it for the majority of my life until this year. I would only use an extended, ported, extra full choke in my Nova and the results were incredible. I have made sixty-yard passing shots at ducks and dropped them dead out of the air. These types of shots we refer to as a "No way" shot. Because when you make a successful shot at this distance and you are with another hunter, the only valid response from them is "No Fucking Way you just hit that!" I sure did, due to my super awesome extended full choke. Just this year I began using an improved and modified choke in my 12-gauge over-under. I decided to make this adult decision while training my new pup, Marcus. This decision came with a lot of thought. I wanted my new pup to know exactly what we were doing. When he hears a gunshot, a bird will fall. I convinced myself that I would only take close shots (inside of thirty yards) so that there was a high probability that the bird would fall in my line of sight and Mark would be able to figure out where the bird went down. When you take a bad shot at fifty yards, you most likely get a crippled bird. Crippled birds are not easy to recover and can sail halfway across the marsh before making a crash landing. I did not want Mark to be disappointed when I made a bad shot and not recover that bird. Mark and I only lost one bird this entire season. That is due to deciding on which chokes to use for the best chance of dropping birds dead instead of cripples. Choosing the right choke tube will help save on ammo and increase the chances of bringing birds home.

AMMO

Ammo can be a difficult choice, depending on who you are. I personally like the Winchester Super X, three-inch, #2 or #4. They are very cheap, reliable, and produce great results, if you know what you are doing. There are hundreds of options of different types of shells with all sorts of different results and price tags. This day and age, I use whatever shells that I can find on the shelf. The best overall waterfowl shell is a 12-gauge three-inch

#2 or #4. You can shoot just about anything you want with that type of shell. Depending on the choke you are using and manufacturer of the shell, you can shoot passing ducks at sixty yards with a four-foot lead. Not the most recommended shot, but it's possible. You can use a three-inch #2 for shooting passing geese at thirty yards or field hunting them at thirty feet from layout blinds. Most hunters will blame a missed bird on the gun or ammo, but I believe it's just your fault and you cannot accept the fact that you missed a perfect shot. I have missed shots that were so close and perfect that I will lose sleep over it. You will constantly be asking yourself, "How the hell did I miss that?" This is where the blame game starts. First question to ask yourself, "Did I flock shoot at those ten Greenheads that were thirty feet away sitting on the water?" Maybe. "It must have been the ammo!" Check to see if there's any steel shot in your pocket from it falling out of the shell before chambering it into your gun. "It had to have been a blank shell, there's no way there was a shot in that shell!" There were most likely hundreds of projectiles in that shell, you just fucked up and missed. Don't blame your gear, blame yourself, become a better shooter!

WADERS

All waterfowl hunters need waders. If you want to get into duck hunting, besides getting your hands on a shotgun and ammo, you must have a pair of waders. Just think about the habitat in which ducks live. You want to be where the ducks live, giving you a better chance at shooting a duck. Ducks like water. People like water too, but only when the water temperatures won't give you hypothermia. When you are pursuing ducks, the water temperatures are very cold. Between the common waterfowl season from October to February the water temperatures are far too cold to stand in the water for hours at a time and live to tell people how fucking cold the water was. At this point waders will keep you warm, dry, and alive, so that you can come back and hunt again.

There are three basic types of waders: neoprene, fishing, and flooded timber style. Neoprene waders are usually the cheapest and are what most people start off with. They are warm and keep the water out, but I highly do not recommend them for jump shooting on the marsh. They are not friendly on the legs after walking many miles and jumping creeks. Most neoprene waders come with an attached built-in boot. When walking in deep mud, the built-in boot tends to stay stuck in the mud and your foot will come out. In this situation you have a 98% chance of falling face first into mud if you are lucky. Worst case scenario, your boot gets stuck, you start to fall forward, brace your fall with the gun you are holding, realize you are in thirty inches of freezing water, with your gun submerged, and your entire body and now your boot is acting as an anchor, holding you in place. You can avoid that whole situation by using fly fishing-style waders. These are the best for walking on the marsh, they come in a lightweight, fully waterproof material and offer an external boot option. Yes, you will still get stuck in mud with these, but when you pull your stuck boot out of the mud, the boot will always come with it. All Orvis fishing waders are great for hunting the marsh. You can layer up under them if you plan to sit in a blind, you can wear shorts under them if you plan on walking many miles. I usually get three years out of a pair of waders before they start to leak. Once a pair of waders start to leak you have two options: clear Flex-Seal or bite the bullet and buy a new pair. Surprisingly, Flex-Seal works very well, but it's not a permanent fix. The last type of waders are what I refer to as flooded timber waders. I'm sure that is the wrong name for them, but I never use them and don't recommend them for jump shooting anyway. These waders have a fancy marsh print on them, look really cool, weigh about forty pounds, and have a built-in boot. They are great if you are standing in cold water all day, but terrible for walking long distances, wading through mud, or anything to do with hunting on the marsh.

CLOTHING AND GEAR

PICKING THE RIGHT GEAR FOR THE APPROPRIATE weather can take a few seasons to figure out. There are thousands of brands out there that do pretty much the same thing: they keep you warm and dry in environments that are cold and wet. During the September early goose season, it's normally in the high 70s and the mosquitos are still out in full force. If you are field hunting geese in layout blinds, you're going to want some gnarly bug spray. I prefer the Muck boots and shorts combo with a long-sleeve t-shirt while I am waiting for birds in my blind. Field hunting in September doesn't require much physical activity once you are hunting. Setting up and breaking down your blinds and decoys takes a little effort, but nothing to complain about. After the September goose season, the temperatures begin to drop, and the good hunting weather starts. During the October waterfowl season when the temperatures are in the 40s, you'll need a good pair of waders, a camo hoodie, and a light rain jacket, if needed. During this time of year, the ducks haven't moved to the salt marshes yet, so during the Central and Coastal seasons, the preferred areas to hunt are the kettle ponds, flooded timber, and tributaries of the Merrimack River. These freshwater areas can be hunted with the same jump shooting style. Instead of navigating the marsh, you are trying to sneak up on ducks while walking through the woods. That may sound easy, but every dry leaf and dead stick makes an extremely loud noise when you step on them. The trick to sneaking up on birds from the woods is simple: don't make any noise or move fast and you can get right up to them. Sometimes I will take twenty minutes to walk 100' trying to get close enough to make a decent shot. Remember the game "Red light, Green light"? That's the best method to use while stalking ducks in the woods. It works really well with diving birds like Hooded Mergansers. When they dive under water, close as much distance as you can and when they pop back up, stop in your tracks and wait. This sometimes works with puddle ducks in flooded timber; this method is more of a "Yellow light" approach. You should be very cautious, walk extremely slow, making as little noise as possible and aiming your next footstep for moss or a fallen log. That is why it may take twenty minutes to cover 100 feet. As November approaches and the temperatures drop farther, you may want to add a nice waterproof jacket on top of your hoodie for an additional layer. But always remember, when you are jump shooting you are always moving, so you do not want to be too hot.

As the temperature drops, the best thing to look for is the skim of ice on the ponds. The ponds will freeze at night and during the day they will thaw. The ducks prefer to sleep in open water, so this gets the ducks flying from saltwater where they roost at night to freshwater where they feed during the day. You would want to hunt your freshwater spot in the late morning as the birds are looking to feed. Then hunt the afternoon low tide on the marsh as the birds are returning to their roost. You need to always think about what the ducks are doing to increase your chances of seeing birds. Late November the ponds tend to freeze solid, and it pushes the traditional puddle ducks—like Wood Ducks and Teal—south, and the resident birds go to the marsh. The most common marsh duck you will encounter is the Black Duck. Black Ducks start to show up on the marshes once the weather begins to get cold. Some Black Ducks show up earlier than others but the majority of them will be here once all the freshwater ponds freeze. December in Massachusetts can bring all sorts of crazy weather. The last few years December has been very mild with winter weather, but the usual temperature range is in the twenties to forties. This is prime salt marsh jump shooting weather. You can still hunt with a hoodie and waders, don't need gloves yet, and not freeze your ass off. All the birds are now in the marshes, and it increases your chances of dedicating all your time to one area instead of bouncing back and forth from freshwater to saltwater.

A face mask is very important while hunting on the marsh. While hunting, most of your skin is covered by some article of clothing except your face. Ducks and geese have extremely good eyesight. By wearing marsh-colored clothes, sometimes they have a hard time picking you up. If you do not have a mask and you stare directly at a bird, they will see you and flare before you even have the thought about taking a shot. This is usually the outcome if you are just walking on the marsh with or without a face mask. If you see a single bird or many birds in flight, try to pick a creek to slide down into or some tall grass, or even lay down completely. This method usually works with geese, they are less spooky. Once geese get up in the morning, they typically fly in one constant direction. If you see geese coming your way, try to find cover. Cover your face and try not to look directly at them. There is a good chance that they will fly close enough for you to get a passing shot. I typically don't hunt with sunglasses unless I am in a blind, they create an unnatural glare, and the birds can pick them out a few hundred yards away.

Gloves are awesome and horrible at the same time. I try to go as long as I can into the season without using them, until it is unbearable to do so. I prefer a thin pair of gloves, something to cut the wind and cold temperature, but not too thick that I do not have to try to take off my trigger glove before taking a shot. Mittens are your warmest option, but terrible for jump shooting. Large winter gloves are the next best for warmth, but you can fumble around trying to find your trigger. I prefer using the half-mitten style glove where you can fold the mitten part backward to expose your bare fingers. All these styles of gloves work great in their own way, until they get wet. Having wet gloves is a great way to ruin your hunt. Trust me, it is easy to get wet gloves while duck hunting; it is pretty much inevitable that your hands are going to enter the water whether you plan on it or not. The best pair of gloves I had for duck hunting were a fly fishing-style half-mitten. They were designed to get wet, but the heat produced by your body warms the wet material and makes it bearable to continue to hunt. Neoprene gloves are great for setting up decoys and that is about it, they are too cumbersome for me to use while shooting.

Having easy access to your shotgun shells is highly recommended. In just about every scenario after you empty your gun, you want to reload as fast as possible. Especially if it was the first two or three shots on the marsh for that morning. If you picked a good spot to jump shoot that morning, once you let that gun sing, you will be amazed by how many birds get up and fly. Sometimes thousands of birds are spooked by the blast and circle in the air. If this is the case, you would want to reload as fast as possible to increase your chances of making another shot. For the last eight years I have been using an external shell pouch. I usually wear it above my waist, that way while walking it doesn't sag too low and hit my legs while I walk. You want those shells to be as close to your reloading position, that way they come right out of the pouch and directly into the gun. If you carry shells in your pockets, it works, but it just takes more time to locate them when time is limited. When carrying shotgun shells on the marsh, especially in an external carrier, you must clean them when you return home. When you clean your gun, clean your shells also. The brass on the shell will rust very quickly. Depending on the amount of rust on a shell, they will still work. Once that primer turns green, there is a small chance that round will fire when you pull the trigger. If the round does fire, there is also a pretty good chance that the shell will get stuck in the chamber. Rusty shells do work, but not all the time. To increase your chances of dropping waterfowl, avoid rusty shells at all costs. It's devastating when you line up a shot on a banded Greenhead, pull the trigger, and the gun goes "click." Now, as the bird begins to fly away, you try to clear that round and the shell is jammed in the chamber. If you cleaned your shells when you put your gun away, this would have never happened.

5

HUNTING THE MARSH AND ITS ENVIRONMENT

NOW THAT YOU HAVE A 12-GAUGE SHOTGUN WITH 3" #2s, a full choke, and a pair of waders, it's time to hit the marsh. Hunting the salt marsh is not as easy as one may think. There are many environmental factors you must consider prior to stepping foot on a salt marsh. The biggest factor that will ruin your day if misjudged, is the tide. Here in Massachusetts the tide cycles every six hours or so. The tide moves about eight feet up and down during those six hours. The most ideal tide for jump shooting the marsh is low tide. At low tide the birds are down in the creeks and you can walk right up to them without them knowing you are there and get a close shot. At high tide ducks and geese will see you coming from 300 yards away and you will never get a shot. Most times I don't even hunt the marsh at high tide. When walking the marsh at low tide you must always remember which direction the open ocean is and which direction the creeks are flowing. This is extremely important because when that tide turns, you need to start heading back toward land. I usually use my waist as a safe zone when crossing creeks with waders. That way if I trip or slip I have about ten inches of water left to catch myself before going under. When crossing creeks at dead low tide there is not much to worry about, you can typically see the bottom of the creek and see what material you are walking on. Always keep in mind how far you have walked, how many creeks you have crossed and how steep the walls are. Some big creeks have ten-feet-high walls with six inches of water in them at low tide. Guess what? Four hours later, that same creek in going to be six feet deep and thirty feet across and may run for five miles winding its way through the marsh. If you end up on the wrong side of that creek on the wrong tide, you will be in for one hell of a night.

I'll explain a scenario. Low tide is at two p.m., sunset is at 4:45 p.m. You start hunting at two-thirty p.m., you should know at this point that the tide has turned and is on the way in. If it took you an hour to walk out, make sure you can make if back before the tide gets too high. Keep this in mind as you walk farther into the marsh. You can typically cross a creek two hours after the low tide change. Some factors that change this are the full moon tides, storm surges, and heavy rainfall. You need to do a little pre-hunt planning prior to attempting to hunt a few hours on the marsh. I usually note the direction of the water in the creeks every fifteen–twenty minutes. Depending on the size of the marsh and your location, the tide shift may differ from the tide chart that you referred to. It is always good to note when slack tide is (when the water stops moving) and when the tide begins to change direction. At this point in time, you should start your journey back to where you started. Other than the tide, you must remember when shooting light is, half hour before sunrise to sunset. If you are out on the marsh a half hour before sunrise, you typically cannot see a damn thing. Some marshes are surrounded by trees, they could be up to a mile away. But when a duck flushes out of the water two minutes after legal shooting, they fly up, and when a Black Duck flies upwards with a dark backdrop before the sun comes up, you can't see shit! Therefore, it is very difficult to take a safe shot at that bird. Most times while jump shooting I will wait until actual sunrise to start jumping creeks on the marsh. It helps to know what you are shooting at and to see where you are walking. Walking on the marsh is a special technique that you can only learn by doing. But I'll do my best to try to help you in what to look out for.

The salt marsh is very unforgiving; there is a reason there are not many permanent structures built on them. It is because they are very unstable, due to only a few species of cord grass with a shallow root system that grows on top of them. While walking on the marsh you need to look out for the length of the grass. Typically, the tall grass indicates water, and lying down grass is safer to walk on. But sometimes the lying down grass is covering a hole that is about fifteen inches across and four feet deep, which creates a recipe for disaster. These are what we refer to as "holes." Said hole can swallow a full-sized adult in a second and if you are by yourself, with an incoming tide and sunset is in an hour and you fall into one of these holes, your future is looking pretty dim at this point. But some holes will only trap a foot. When I am teaching new people to walk / hunt on the marsh I tell them to just take a knee when they find themselves sinking or falling into a hole. Trust me, you'll understand when you start to sink, it's much easier to recover from the kneeling position than when one leg is buried four feet in a hole. Just remember, tall grass = bad; short grass = better, but still could be bad.

The ever-deceptive Salt Panne. Avoid these at all costs, unless you drop a bird in the middle. Do not try to cross them because the distance is shorter to walk. A salt panne is essentially a saltwater pond in the middle of the marsh. They somehow hold water, and they make for the most unreliable walking platform on this planet. They normally appear to have six inches or less of water in them. But below that six inches of water is about fifty inches of mud, or sometimes three inches of mud, there is absolutely no way of knowing how deep that mud is. Sometimes you can walk nearly all the way across, building confidence that this is not one of the ones that I'm talking about (that author was full of shit) then your next step lands you in four feet of mud and that pocket your phone was safely in is now submerged in water. Now in panic mode, you know that the ninety feet of salt panne behind you is mostly good, but you see hard land fifteen feet in front of you. Which way do you chose to go in that situation? Here's a fun fact. Don't fucking walk across a salt panne in the first place. Go around it.

Yup, this is a salt panne, try walking across it, I dare you!

Mud

THERE ARE DOZENS OF DIFFERENT TYPES OF MUD throughout the marsh: Regular mud, dark mud, light mud, mud that looks like diarrhea, mud that looks like sand, sand that looks like mud, hard mud, soft mud, ankle-deep mud, knee-deep mud, oh-shit mud, frozen mud, and bottomless mud. Regular mud is typically four inches to six inches deep and is easily navigable with a good pair of waders. Dark mud—you need to be careful—it is usually at the bottom of a creek with a foot of water on top and there is no way of knowing how deep it is going to be. Light mud is usually very soft; very soft mud is typically at least knee deep and usually about halfway up the bank, it will really give you a run for your money when trying to climb out of a creek. Sand. Sand is normally good for walking on because of its density, when walking through a creek at low tide, the sand usually accumulates where the water is flowing and 75% of the time you won't sink in it when walking. But there is also mud that looks like sand. After walking for fifty yards in knee deep mud, your legs are going to be smoked—burning and on fire. A nice sand bar appears as you round the corner, it is a little out of the way, but it gives you hope for potentially easier navigation. Your confidence tells you that it's going to be a hard platform that you can start walking normally again and give your thighs a break. Nope! Not today, that's mud that looks like sand! And guess what, you are now farther from your destination, in deeper mud and the tide is coming in. You'll know exactly what I'm talking about when you put yourself in this situation. "Oh-shit mud" is kind of a general category for all types of mud, when you step into it and your first reaction in "Oh shit!" That, my friend, is oh-shit mud.

Frozen salt water can freeze completely solid or partially solid. Every footstep is a mystery. Now, those ever-deceptive salt pannes, they appear to freeze solid and look like you could ice skate on them. Be very careful when walking across these, they are just as dangerous as when they are in a liquid state. This salt-infused ice can hold you, but the next step could land you balls deep in mud as one leg breaks through the ice resulting in a highly uncomfortable position. As you crawl out of this position, most likely gloves soaking wet, gun filled with muddy salt water, you will think to yourself, "Fuck, that author told me not once, but twice, that this was going to happen."

Frozen mud. Let me tell you a story about frozen mud. I went out for an afternoon jump shoot on the marsh in Salisbury. This was the first time in a few weeks I was able to get out for a hunt. Just prior to this hunt, we had a serious cold stretch in the area, it was at most, twenty-five degrees or less for over five days. Everything was frozen, including the marsh. When the marsh freezes, it creates an unstable, partially frozen, walking platform. The frozen mud to look out for is about twelve inches to eighteen inches below the grass level as you step down into a creek. Let me explain a step-by-step scenario of how frozen mud can absolutely rock your world in less than one second. What is known as "jumping creeks," you either jump over them or drop down into them and cross to get to the other side. When you drop down into them at low tide, the creek bank walls are on average between four feet and ten feet high. When approaching a creek, you will want to stop and look for the best and easiest way to step down into them. This is where you run into different layers and densities of mud. Typically, the upper one–three feet on mud is most stable because it has some sort of root system in it making it a little bit more stable to hold weight. But not every time. With my years of marsh walking education and training, I confidently stepped onto a root ball, thinking it looked good and was already eyeing my next step. Well, it didn't go the way I planned. I stepped down on this fully frozen root ball with my left foot, which instantaneously slipped out from under me. Because I had 100% committed to putting all my weight on that root ball, I was now freefalling backward, but downward at the same time. Now, we can't forget about my right foot, that was still on somewhat solid ground back up at the grass level. So, as I fall backward and downward, the first thing that makes contact is my spine, directly on that good-for-nothing frozen ball of mud and roots.

Still at this point in time, my right foot is somewhere up near my head which is ringing from a 240-pound drop to solid ice. Now gravity kicks my ass some more after I come to a stop. The elasticity of my entire right leg that is somehow above and behind me, preloaded my body for launch, headfirst downward another four feet into ten inches of thirty-degree water and eight inches of mud. With my head ringing, gun submerged in mud, laying in the bottom of the creek wondering what the fuck just happened, Mark comes over to lick my face to make sure I'm alive. I gather myself, empty my gun out, slowly stand up, and the first thing I looked at was that solid frozen root ball and say to myself, "Motherfucker!"

A decent size creek, low tide is twelve inches deep, high tide over six feet deep.

FOR A PERFECT DAY HUNTING ON THE MARSH, the following environmental factors would exist: a late morning low tide, say 8:30 a.m., slightly overcast / snow, ten–fifteen mph wind and about twenty-five degrees. I'll explain why each of these matters. Having a low tide at eight-thirty a.m. gives you more opportunity to hunt the tide than a 6:45 low tide. As I mentioned before, two hours before and after the low tide are the safest tide to hunt. As the tide goes out and comes back in, you will most likely be able to cross the creek to get back to the truck. My average jump shoot takes about two–three hours and I usually cover two or three miles of marsh. If you are two miles from safety and you misjudge the timing of the tide, you will be in serious trouble.

Cloud cover to block the sun is the best-case scenario. It does not help during those thirty minutes prior to sunrise, but through the day you will not have to battle the sun blinding you as you jump birds out of the creek. Please take my word for it and don't even bother jump shooting ducks if you have to aim into the sun, it's very dangerous and you have no idea what type of bird it is that you are about to shoot. In Massachusetts there is only one type of duck that you cannot shoot and that is a Harlequin. These birds are known as Sea Ducks and are primarily found off of Andrews Point in Rockport feeding in the surf. I'm not saying they won't be in the marsh, but it is a pretty good chance you don't have to worry about shooting one on the marsh. That being said, there are other birds and animals that you cannot shoot while engaged in waterfowl hunting, such as Great Blue Herons or Whitetail deer. Both of these animals can be seen on the salt marsh at any given time. So, if you are sneaking up on a creek at low tide and the sun is blocking your direct line of sight, all you really have for senses at this point are your ears. When ducks blast out of a creek you can hear the splash of the water and a fast-paced wing beat as the duck flies vertically upward then onward. When you spook a Great Blue Heron out of a creek and all you hear is wing beats, but you cannot see shit as you shoulder your gun, you may want to re-think the situation you have put yourself in. Don't walk into the sun while jump shooting.

Hunting in the snow: My dad always told me that there is nothing like duck hunting during a snowstorm. If you get the opportunity to hunt the salt marsh during an eight-thirty a.m. low tide during a snowstorm, it won't get any better. One of the best factors of hunting in the snow is that it muffles noise. Ducks are very smart; their only defenses are their senses. If they see you, they will fly away. If they hear you, they will fly away. And when they fly away, they are so fast that you must be within thirty yards and have about a second to determine how you will successfully shoulder your gun, aim with a lead, and pull the trigger before it is too late. Hesitation will cost you many opportunities to successfully put birds on the ground. When you are sneaking up on a creek, take your time! If you walk up to that creek too fast and make too much noise, those ducks will hear you from 100 yards out and you will never get an opportunity to take a shot. Every single creek has the potential for holding a bird, or many birds. Creeks come in all different shapes and sizes. They can be 100 feet wide or one foot wide and still hold birds. So, when sneaking up on a creek you should be expecting the potential for birds to be in it. The feeling is like no other. Your heart rate will be up; it will feel like it is in your throat. Nervous and excited, loaded with adrenaline but calm, you need to be quiet. You know the feeling when you slip on ice and you're not sure if you are about to totally eat shit or catch yourself and you get that crazy feeling throughout your entire body for a split second? Well, if you are doing everything right when sneaking up on a creek, that is the feeling you should have in your body as you slowly approach the bank. The snow can muffle your footsteps, creating the perfect opportunity to get as close to these incredibly intelligent birds so you can improve your chances of bringing home a bird. If there is a decent head wind, plus some snow, the ducks are usually flying low. Low flying duck = no flying duck. Always remember to check directly below you in the creek when you get to the edge. Some birds may be up against the bank you are standing on. They may not have heard you approach if they had their heads under water while feeding. I have had it happen many times when I stop five feet from the bank and don't see a bird. Then I let my guard down and a pair of Black Ducks blast out from below my feet and because I'm not paying attention they flew away. I'm not saying drop down into the creek to look, but just stick your head over the bank and take a look.

6

Duck Hunting

AT THIS POINT IN YOUR MARSH HUNTING experience, we have covered what gear you should have as well as where and when you can hunt. That's the most important part of getting ready to attempt duck hunting. What we have not covered yet are retrieval methods. There are many ways to retrieve dead or crippled birds and I will go over the basics. The most common method of retrieving a bird is on foot. It is definitely not the most successful, but it works. You are just very limited to water depth, creek size and width, holes, trenches, tall and short grass, and everything else that may prevent you from getting that bird. When you shoot a bird, please try to watch where that bird goes down. It is easy to do if only one bird flushes. But when you flush nine ducks and you flock shoot your first shot and miss, now you let them get farther away, you focus on a specific bird, pull the trigger, watch it fold. Depending on the gun you have, you may have a third shot. Now you are on to the next bird that is now pushing forty-five yards, but since you have an extra full choke in, you can reach out and tap that bird also. Because it was a far shot, the bird comes down crippled and soars another seventy yards away.

"Holy shit! That was awesome! But where the hell are my birds? I don't even remember where that first one dropped, I think I know where that second one is, but it may be 100 yards from the first one."

You must give an honest effort to look for those birds; it is actually a law here in Massachusetts called Wanton Waste. You must make a reasonable effort to retrieve and use the animal. If you think that when you shoot a duck, that you can just walk over to it, pick it up, and go about your hunt, you are badly mistaken. Retrieving birds can be that easy, but it does not happen every time. I have spent hours on my hands and knees crawling through marshes and swamps looking for birds and wishing there was a better way. Guess what? There is one. They are known as dogs, and they are absolutely life changing when retrieving birds.

I grew up with duck hunting dogs; my dad always had a dog that would retrieve birds for us. They were never professionally trained, but they would get birds for me whenever I couldn't. They are amazing and there is nothing like watching your own dog, that you have most likely trained, work for a bird after you pulled the trigger. Two years ago, my wife got me a puppy for Christmas. She knew I always wanted a duck hunting dog and sure enough got me one. His name is Marcus. He's a beautiful male Golden Retriever. The day we brought him home I had already made a toy for him, a duck wing tied to a stick. That is how my grandfather and father trained their duck dogs and that is all I knew going into training Mark. He had natural retriever instincts, and we trained every single day. I read one book but other than that had absolutely no idea what I was doing; but he did. We trained almost every day from January to October. I trained him under the command of the word "Duck." Whenever he hears the word "Duck," he stops in his tracks and looks at me. He knows exactly what "Duck" is. "Duck" means he gets to hunt. This season was the best season I have ever had. I only shot about a dozen or so ducks, but every duck I dropped was a hundred times more rewarding than any other bird I have ever retrieved. When Mark hears a gunshot followed by the word "Duck" he knows it's business time and that he needs to find the bird and bring it back to me. I specifically chose to use my over-under Stevens 555 12 gauge. I had an improved choke on the top barrel and a modified choke on the bottom. The improved choke was great for shots within twenty yards and the modified would successfully reach out to thirty-five yards. I made this choice for a few reasons. This gun was very light and because Mark had to be held on a leash his first year. I could never two-hand carry while jump shooting. I always had Mark on my left side and my gun on my right. Having only two shots instead of three with my Nova, I feel like it made me a better shooter. I focused on every shot. I also switched out my chokes from full to make sure I made a good ethical shot so that Mark would know that when he hears a shot followed by the common "Duck," a bird was on the ground. That season we only lost one bird, and compared to every season prior, that was incredible.

If a dog is not an option, the next best thing is a twelve-foot canoe. Before my wife got me Marcus for Christmas, I primarily hunted from a canoe. Hunting from a canoe is almost as good as hunting with a dog, it's just far more work. I started hunting from a kayak. I highly do not recommend that, but if it's your only option, it will work. Kayaks are usually very light and low in the water which make for good portable blinds but only if they are stationary. Shooting from a moving kayak is extremely dangerous. Shooting straight in front is not that bad but as soon as you have to swing left or right it gets extremely tippy. You also have to crotch a loaded shotgun and paddle over the top. So, if you are jump shooting birds, the first thing you will do is drop your kayak paddle on top of your gun. Now you have to bring your gun over your paddle and at this point I can almost guarantee that bird is not directly in front of you. You are now swinging on that bird in the middle of the water. Highly focused on that bird, you don't know how far you are leaning on the boat and then you let off a shot. If you thought your balance was off before, think again! If your only option is a kayak, spray paint it a flat green and brown, and use a canoe paddle. After having too many close calls in a nine-foot kayak, I upgraded to a thirteen-foot canoe. This thirteen-foot canoe was a complete game changer. I saw this canoe on the side of the road with a "For sale" sign on it with no price. I knocked on the door and a ninety-year-old woman answered the door. I asked how much she was selling the canoe for, and she said "$40 and its yours!" I gave her the $40 and thanked her. She said as I was loading it up, "I hope you get some good use out of it!" If only she knew now how many adventures and lifetime memories that $40 boat has given me and others ... Any canoes thirteen feet and under are very hard to find, especially for $40. This was a Grumman canoe; brand new they are over $1000! This one was probably from the 1970s or '80s and needed a little love. That night I took it home and I slapped on a coat of Rustoleum Topsider Forest Green paint, and she looked beautiful. The following morning, I had to take her out hunting. The paint was still tacky and soft, but I didn't even hesitate. As soon as I put it in the bed of my truck, about three feet of fresh paint scraped off the bottom. I thought to myself, "I'm going to be beating the ever-living shit out of this thing. She still looks great with this glossy paint job but will look even better covered in mud with a bird on the deck." This canoe changed the game; I could get into places I've dreamt about hunting my whole life. Hunting without a boat limits your ability to hunting the marsh at low tide only. You can hunt at any tide, but the probability of shooting a bird is low and retrieving one at high tide is very unlikely. Now with this canoe I can hunt at any tide. The preferred tide to hunt with a canoe is any level of tide that your head does not stick out above the marsh. It is easier to sneak up on birds this way. If you can see them, they can see you. Jump shooting the marsh works best when you and the birds are both surprised when you see each other.

The best $40 I have ever spent, my 13-foot Grumman canoe.

OVER YEARS OF CANOE HUNTING, I DIALED IN MY focus on how to use the canoe in the best way possible and here are my recommendations. Always wear a life jacket; here in Massachusetts it is required by law that, between September 15 and May 15, you must wear a life jacket at all times. The reason for this is that if you fall into the water during this time of year, there's a pretty good chance you could die from hypothermia. I would recommend an auto-inflate style PFD. They are less bulky and don't get in the way when you shoulder your gun. There is a known rumor that if you fall off of a boat with waders on you are going to sink and die. If you are wearing waders on a canoe and you are wearing your PFD, you are not going to die. I have been canoe hunting for nine years now and have never had a close call from falling in. When I take out my canoe, I always have a canoe dolly, PFD, and two paddles. I covered the gunnels with rubber hose so that when I hit the metal boat with a wood paddle it muffles the noise. A canoe dolly is a must if you have to drag a canoe filled with gear over fifty feet. With my canoe, I can fit five dozen Divebomb goose silhouettes, five dozen Mallard silhouettes, eight duck floaters on a jerk rig, and a few goose floaters. That's a great set up for one hell of a solo hunt. I've only done it a few times, but it is possible. I prefer packing out light: canoe, two paddles, my over-under 12 gauge, and a dozen shells. The most important item when waterfowl hunting out of a canoe is that second paddle. Besides a backup if you break one, the second paddle allows you to drop the primary paddle in the water and pick up your gun to take a shot. I have tried to tie off a paddle, but it always gets tangled. I've tried to drop it in the boat, but it is far too loud. If you are silently paddling around a bend of a creek in the kneeling position and there are birds facing away from you, you can gently release the paddle into the water and in the same motion, silently pick up your shotgun that is resting in a safe direction within arm's reach. Now you are one step ahead of those birds. You take your shot and drop a bird. If you are in the position I'm describing, your bird will most likely be floating dead in the creek ahead of you. Keep an eye on that bird, grab your second paddle and go get your bird, and then go retrieve your primary paddle. It can be easy to forget about that paddle you dropped before you took the shot. Canoe hunting works with two people, either two canoes or two people in one canoe. If you are hunting two people to a canoe, I would recommend only one person shooting at a time. Preferably the person sitting in front would have both hands on their gun and is ready to shoot at any moment. It's a great spot for the person in the front. If you are the one paddling, you're going to want your shotgun pointed in a safe direction, which would be to the left or right. With the gun pointed in this direction, it is difficult to manipulate the paddle without hitting it. I would highly suggest just unloading your shotgun while going tandem. Take turns between being the shooter and the paddler. The boat will be much easier to control this way and it is almost guaranteed that the shooter will get a great shot when sneaking around a corner.

My brother enjoys canoe hunting for deer on the marsh and is extremely successful at it. He will normally hunt solo at a three-quarter tide where his head is at the same level as the marsh and sneak up on big bucks with his muzzleloader. This one time, he took a friend out with him on his seventeen-foot canoe. Two full-size adults and gear. They shot a deer on the marsh, loaded it into the canoe, and then started to head back to the truck. What he didn't do was check the weather prior to going out. Something you should always do before hunting, is always check the weather, not just for the morning when you arrive at your hunting spot, but for the entire day. They were in this seventeen-foot canoe, loaded down with two geared up adults and a 200-pound deer with a 350-yard paddle across an open bay. The wind picked up and the waves were growing. You don't need a big wave when you have ten inches of freeboard left on a fully loaded canoe. The wind was blowing them away from shore and the waves were starting to fill the boat with water. I also forgot to mention that this was in December on the ocean in Massachusetts. My brother told me that was one of the scariest hunting trips of his life because he knew that if they flipped the canoe there was no way they would have survived the swim to shore.

Canoe hunting The Great Marsh for Deer.

They both paddled as hard as they could into the waves and didn't give up. They aimed for the closest shoreline and paddled literally for their lives. Once they got to land, they dragged the canoe in silence to the trucks, loaded the canoe and deer in silence, and departed in silence. I introduced that friend to my brother and that was their first day meeting and hunting together. Throughout your life you will find many hunting partners, people you like to go hunting with or try to go hunting with. You will know during the first hunt whether you will call them back for another hunt or never again. The most important thing to look for while hunting with someone else is, safety. You should be asking yourself this question: "If I continue to hunt with this person will I make it home by the end of the day?" If you ever doubt the other persons safety at any moment, call them out immediately. Do not hesitate to express your concerns of safety when hunting, you may never get another chance.

7

DUCK AND GOOSE CALLING

DUCK CALLING CONFIDENCE: THERE IS ALWAYS a better caller when hunting in a group. Everyone always waits for that one person to start calling, just to determine if they are going to attempt to call or not. It is an unspoken rule among all hunters. I just recently became a decent caller, thanks to Nate Walker of Hank Walker Decoys in Newbury, MA. He makes custom wood calls and recently taught a class on calling techniques. It takes years to practice and get right. Calling ducks while jump shooting is almost a waste of time; well for me it is, because by the time I get two shots off, every duck in the entire marsh is in the air frantically flying around looking for a place to land. But they can see you and don't want anything to do with your position. That's my experience with calling ducks while jump shooting.

Most waterfowl hunters who hunt on the marsh typically use floating style decoys; this method is much easier than jump shooting. Easier, as in you throw out the decoys, rip some duck calls, and wait for the birds to come to you. Sometimes the birds just aren't flying that morning and that's when you can go for a jump shoot. Jump shooting is the complete opposite, it's about the element of surprise, you have to go find the birds and that may take you on a three-to-five-mile round trip of jumping creeks and navigating the marsh. When Kagan (my best friend and hunting partner) and I first started hunting this area together, we both always carried calls with us, but never knew how to use them. They make for a hell of a good picture regardless of if you know how to use them or not.

Custom duck call lanyard I made engraved with all the names of outdoorsmen who inspire me, a Green Wing Teal and my over under.

Calling geese, on the other hand, works very well when they are in small numbers, especially singles. Once you master just the single honk out of your goose call, you will be able to turn a single goose toward you. My favorite method of calling single honkers is to let out four to six honks to get its attention. Once that bird starts flying in your direction and honking, you now have its attention. Wait for the bird to start calling out to other birds, then go honk for honk. You honk, the bird honks, you honk, the bird honks. This should get the bird close enough to take a thirty-yard passing shot at it. I mentioned earlier that you want to understand where waterfowl like to roost and typically go during the day. Early season, birds normally roost in the marsh and fly to freshwater or fields during the day to feed. As the temperatures get colder, the ponds get covered with ice and fields covered with snow. The behavior of the waterfowl changes. With a cold winter, by December most of the birds are on the marsh. Ducks always fly first thing in the morning; they usually start to move from a half hour before sunrise to sunrise, which is a great time to set up a half dozen decoys and start calling. Geese, on the other hand, typically fly between seven a.m. and nine a.m.; they will continue to fly around the marsh all day but most fly during that time frame. On your morning commute to and from work, keep an eye out for geese from September to February and note the time that you see them flying. Once you practice this, you will have a better understanding of where and when to target them. Geese usually roost on the marsh by the thousands; they have a pretty good routine every single day. The only thing that changes this routine is extreme weather. They may have to hunker down for a day if the wind is greater than thirty-five mph. Geese are very large birds and struggle flying into the wind. Although, if they are flying into the wind within shooting range, take full advantage of it when you can. If a goose that weighs twelve pounds is flying head-on into forty mph winds, they can't make much headway. But keep in mind how fast the wind is blowing and if it is a far shot you will have to lead the bird a little because the wind will blow your shot behind the bird before it reaches it. You only have to worry about this with forty-five-plus yards long shots in forty-five mph wind. If you don't know what forty-five mph wind is, ask yourself, "Should I even be out hunting in this?" That's probably at least forty mph.

Okay, I'll get back to calling geese soon. Goose hunting on the marsh in the morning can be successful, but it is not the ideal time to target them. Around seven a.m. the geese start to fly toward the fields to eat. Whatever marsh that you are hunting on, you will want to do a little research prior to the hunt and study where the closest farms are and what types of crops they have grown there. Whether it is corn, vegetables, or hay. This is important because of the time of year and growing season. Geese prefer corn over everything else, but depending on if we had a dry or rainy year that depends on when the farmer cut the fields. Typically, during a drought, the farmers will cut their corn the first week of September and early season geese are going to target those fields first. But during a wet year, the farmers may let their crops grow into October to get the biggest yield. This directs early season birds toward vegetable and hay fields. I would highly recommend finding a private farm and getting written permission from the landowner to hunt geese on it. It is far more successful than pass shooting them on the marsh. As the season gets further into the winter and the corn gets picked clean by birds and deer, the geese begin to look for late season food, usually in hay fields and along the tide line on the edges of open marsh.

So, now that you understand where geese are going to feed and why, this will help you understand where to set up on the marsh either in the morning or evening to try to be more successful at dropping some geese. If you are doing a morning jump shoot, it is easier to retrieve all birds when shot at low tide; it is also easier to hide at low tide. When you start to see the flight pattern of early morning geese, try to position yourself directly below them and hide to try and get a passing shot. This will be the most successful method of hunting geese in the morning on the marsh. That is because there are usually 5,000 or more geese in a big roost. They get up during that two-to-three-hour window and begin flying to the fields in flocks of twenty-five to fifty or more. If you are set up with a dozen decoys and a blind on the marsh these geese do not want to land back on the marsh, they want to go eat and that is what they are going to do. Morning goose decoys do work, they will attract geese over close enough to come take a look and if you're really lucky you'll get them to commit and land in your spread. But the majority of the birds are heading in one direction, toward food. If you don't have any decoys and you start to notice the flight path, try to get as close as you can to it, and start looking for single geese. They are the easiest to manipulate with a goose call. The big flocks usually won't respond to calling without decoys. Now, if you are set up in those fields where they are heading, you'll be in for an awesome morning. Geese usually fly from field to field throughout the day, sometimes they stay in one all day—depends on the geese, environmental conditions, and predators.

The most successful goose hunting that I have had is in cornfields for an afternoon / sunset hunt. These geese try to feed before they go to roost back on the marsh and start feeding about an hour before sunset. If you do not have permission to hunt a corn field and the marsh is your only option, you're going to want to scout the area during this time and see where the geese are roosting. They usually like a "safe space" so they do not have to worry much about predators during the night. These "safe spaces" are never near a wood line; they are usually in the middle of the marsh on or near a salt panne. This would be a great place to set up with some decoys, a powerful goose call, and a portable layout blind. Some geese go to these fields to feed before bed, but some come in early and if you are in the right place at the right time, you should have much success when calling and decoying geese on a sunset hunt on the marsh.

Shooting Distances

THIS IS SOMETHING THAT TAKES YEARS OF TRIAL and error. There is not a good way to practice this except by doing it. Learning and judging how far a bird is to deliver the most effective shot is hard to do. There are a few things that you need to learn. How to identify the species of bird on the wing (while flying) and how far your gun can effectively shoot. If the bird is too close, with a full choke there won't be anything left; too far of a shot and your crippled goose will coast 2,000 yards to a crash landing in a different town. Depending on the species of bird and its size, that will give you an indication of how far away it is. Geese are a great example to use because of their size. If you can see their feet and eyes, let it rip; that bird is most likely within thirty yards. This is one of those skills that you'll need to develop over time. There is something called "patterning your gun" and I honestly don't really know how to do it, but a lot of hunters do this prior to the season. You can't use a rangefinder on a duck that is flying by at fifty mph, so you need to become good at judging distances.

8

TYPES OF WATERFOWLS SPECICES ON THE MARSH

IT HAS TAKEN ME ALMOST TWO DECADES OF waterfowl hunting to be able to 100% identify every type of bird that you may see when jump shooting on the marsh. When my dad first learned how to hunt in the late '60s and early '70s he didn't have much but a pair of L.L.Bean boots, blue jeans, and maybe a jacket. He has never owned a decoy or a duck call. He also got to waterfowl hunt during the time when you could use lead shot to shoot ducks and geese. Another famous quote I grew up hearing as a kid from him was, "Boys, nothing drops a goose like 00 Buck; There's never any cripples!" My dad also has it out for shooting geese, he prefers shooting a passing goose over a duck any day. He has ONLY shot at passing geese; to my knowledge he has never shot decoying geese in a field. I look forward to the day I can show him how to do it. Back to his knowledge of identifying a duck on the wing, this was his method of doing it.

When I started duck hunting at age twelve the daily limit for Black Ducks was one per day. The Mallard limit changes every few years between two and four. One and two can be female, respectively. If we went out for a jump shoot and in the first five minutes shot a Black Duck, the hunt was over, and we went home. If we shot a hen Mallard when the limit was two, we would end the hunt and go home. After many years of this, I started to look in the flock for a greenhead and selectively aim at him first. That way if I dropped him, I could take another shot at whatever was left. As I made progress with my duck identifying skills, I took a state sponsored waterfowl ID course and that really brought it to a whole new level. I got some great waterfowl ID books and studied them whenever I could. I highly recommend getting a good waterfowl ID book with real pictures and keep it in your primary vehicle with a good pair of binoculars. This way any time you see any type of waterfowl you look at them and verify the species in your waterfowl ID guide. If you make this common practice in the off season, you'll be a pro at identifying duck species while hunting. Identifying a sitting duck is not very difficult; glass it with some binoculars and then check the guide. But what happens when this duck is flying by you at forty mph, thirty yards away in a group of ten other ducks and there are two different species of duck in the group, and you already have one Black Duck in your bag? Now you have a problem if you have no idea how to identify a duck "on the wing."

The most common species of waterfowl you will see on the Great Marsh are the Black Duck, Canada Goose, Hooded Merganser, Bufflehead, and Mallard. There are plenty of other types of waterfowl to potentially encounter while jump shooting too. There are roughly twenty or more different waterfowl species that you could get a shot at during the season on the Great Marsh. The marsh holds two different types of ducks: the puddle duck and the diving duck. There are also other birds that you may encounter while jump shooting that are not a game bird and should not be shot, like the Common Loon. Loons have diving duck characteristics, but it is illegal to shoot them because they are not considered a federal migratory game bird. Another bird you may see is a Grebe; there are a few different species of Grebes, and you should study what those look like, so you do not accidently shoot one. Great Blue Herons will surprise the shit out of you too. Don't shoot those! Another common hunting identification mistake is shooting a Mute Swan, thinking it is a Snow Goose. A Snow Goose is about a quarter of the size of a swan, with a wingspan of about thirty inches and weight around six or seven pounds. The Mute Swan is the closest thing to a Pterodactyl that you're ever going to see, with a wingspan of over six feet and weighing almost forty pounds. There is no way they should be confused with a Snow Goose. If you ever decide to hunt rail or snipe, make sure that you are 100% positive about your identification of these two species. The rail is a very unique bird and does not look like most shore birds, but when hunting them, they are surrounded by shorebirds that are most likely endangered or protected in some way; just be careful! The common snipe looks like a long-legged Woodcock but live on the saltmarsh. I have only ever encountered one or two of these birds and it's usually during early goose season when I am jump shooting with a 10 gauge, so I don't even bother shouldering my gun because both snipe and rail probably do not weigh more than a pound and there would not be much bird left. This year was the first year I tried to hunt rail with no success, but I was 100% confident on the identification of a common rail before attempting to hunt them. The shorebird known as Yellowlegs and the Willet could be easily confused with the common snipe to the uneducated hunter. After you have mastered the identification of all birds, then try to hunt the snipe and rail. The Harlequin is the only duck species that is prohibited to hunt in Massachusetts. You can find them off of Andrews Point feeding in the surf during the winter. I would highly suggest learning their identification, so you know what not to shoot if one comes in with a group of Sea Ducks.

Now let's get into the ones you can shoot! While

on the marsh the most common duck you will see is the Black Duck. These birds are native to the area and typically spend their winters in and around the Great Marsh. They leave and fly north to Canada in the spring and raise their young. Toward the end of the year, they fly south along the Atlantic Ocean and thrive throughout the winter. Black Ducks are called Black Ducks because they are a very dark brown and black color; they can be confused with a hen Mallard on the wing but when you place them next to each other, you can easily tell the difference between the two. Black Ducks are usually bigger than Mallards, which is another way to tell the difference between them. They can be found in flocks of all Black Ducks or mixed in with some Mallards or other puddle ducks. So, when shooting into a flock of Mallards and Black Ducks, you will need to be able to positively identify the difference between the two, especially if you have two Black Ducks already in your bag, which is the daily limit. Black Ducks can mate with a Mallard and create a hybrid duck. The males can sometime be identified with a few green feathers on the head or the secondaries on the wing will have a white wing bar above and below the speculum of the wing. If you shoot a hybrid Black / Mallard, you want to count it toward the most limited species which is the Black Duck. Say you jump a pair of Black Ducks out of a creek. Retrieve both and think you have a hybrid, you will count that as a Black Duck and your daily Black Duck bag limit has been met.

On December 22, 2022, Marcus made his first double Black duck retrieve.

MALLARDS

Mallards are amazing ducks. Although they are an introduced species, they make for an excellent game bird. I believe they came over from Europe at some point in the past and now call North America home. The drake Mallard is one of the top three most beautiful ducks, in my opinion. They have so many colorations of feathers, when examined closely you appreciate how amazing these birds are. The Mallard daily bag limit seems to change throughout the years between two and four Mallards per day. This is determined by the federal government, depending on the nesting season. Drought plays a big factor in waterfowl nesting habitats. If there is a dry year the birds are limited to less nesting habitat and predation, lowering the number of successful broods of new chicks. In a dry year, or consecutive dry years, the Mallard limit will decrease to prevent over harvest from hunting. Although Mallards and Black Ducks are very similar in size, they have completely different characteristics. Black Ducks seem to be shyer than Mallards. They spook much more easily. I have also heard that Black Ducks only decoy into Black Duck decoys, where Mallards will decoy into both Black and Mallard decoys. So, when buying decoys for the marsh it's always good to have a nice set of Black Duck decoys. Mallards can be found on almost any body of water; they are in flooded timber, rivers, potholes, and commonly found on the marsh. The Mottled duck looks just like a hen

Mallard and Black Duck, they are not a hybrid species but are very uncommon in the area of the Great Marsh.

WOOD DUCK

The Wood Duck or "Woody" is the most beautiful drake you may ever see. Personally, I have a place in my heart for Woodies. The reason why is that when I went hunting with Mark on his first day, I shot an absolute stud of a drake Woody, and it was his first duck ever. He made a great retrieve once he understood the assignment and brought that bird right back to my feet. I was so proud of him for doing that for me and it created this bond between the two of us that is too difficult to explain with words. Wood Ducks are most commonly found in freshwater, mostly flooded timber and beaver ponds. Once the temperatures start to drop and the ponds begin to freeze, they head south and skip the salt marsh all together. You can find them on the marsh but not for very long as the temperatures begin to fall. I only have two taxidermy ducks and that is one of them. That Woody is my first dog's first bird and that can never happen again in this life, so that is the reason for the mount. Some hunters like to mount a drake of every species they shoot, and that would be the dream, but in reality, it is very expensive, and you have to have a place to put them all. My other mount is a Longtail formally known as an "Oldsquaw." I like to have my birds mounted in the standing position instead of flying. If they are standing you can save some space and put them on a shelf and whenever you want to admire their pure beauty, you just pick them up and take a look. Wood Ducks are also extremely delicious, but we will get into that later.

Mark's first duck.

THE GREEN-WINGED TEAL

These birds are very fun to target, as one of the smallest

species of duck that you will encounter on the marsh and flooded timber. These birds usually hang out in large flocks in freshwater ponds in the early season, then head to the marsh after the ponds lock up with ice. They are extremely fast and cut in crazy directions when attempting to land or take off. They are not very easily spooked so you can get close to them while jump shooting. They also don't fly very far, so pay attention to where they land, and you may have another chance at jumping them. The Green-winged Teal drake is another beautiful bird, but you will not see full plumage drakes until late in the winter when these birds are on the marsh. Early season they look almost identical to the hens. Always check your daily bag limits as they can change from year to year, but you can normally shoot six Green-winged Teal in your daily bag. Within the first week of central duck season, you may be lucky enough to get a shot at a Blue-winged Teal, they are just about identical to the Green-winged Teal ... I wonder what the difference is. That's right! One has a blue wing, and one has a green wing! The drakes have noticeably different breeding plumage. But the Blue-winged Teal only sticks around in the first or second week of October and then they will head south and skip the marsh. There are other types of Teal that do exist but are uncommon in this area, like the Cinnamon Teal; they are most common in the Pacific Flyway.

Early season Green-wing Teal canoe hunt.

THE SHOVELER

I have never shot at one or even seen one while duck hunting. I have seen plenty of them during the duck season but in an area where I cannot legally shoot them, such as Parker River Wildlife Refuge. Sundays are great for bringing your waterfowl identification guide, a pair of binoculars, and a decent camera to Parker River to learn about birds. There are always hundreds of different species of birds that you can study throughout the year, like ducks and geese, swans, mergansers, grebes, loons, dozens of species of shorebirds, birds of prey, pheasants, turkeys, and countless songbirds. Being able to identify these types of birds will help you become a better hunter, mostly to stay out of trouble. It also helps educate you throughout the off season and gives you something to do. But Shovelers are a very odd-looking duck and about the size of a Wood Duck.

AMERICAN WIDGEON

The American Widgeon is another bird I have not had the pleasure to shoot, but they are fairly common in the northern portion of the Great Marsh, commonly found from the Northern area of Rowley to Woodbridge Island in Newbury. This area is difficult to jump shoot because of its size. As the crow flies, it's about four miles, but if you could possibly walk this distance, you would put in over fifty miles of jumping creeks. The best method to hunt this area is with a boat and some good decoys. These birds tend to appear in the December and January months.

GADWALL

Though the Gadwall can be found in this area, I would consider them less than common. I have shot a half dozen over the years; they are also referred to as a Gray Duck.

The drakes have mostly gray colored feathers but when examined closely the feathers are surprisingly ornate and beautiful. The hens look like a small hen Mallard.

MERGANSERS

There are three types of mergansers that you will encounter during a jump shoot of the marsh. Most new duck hunters have most of their success with Hooded Mergansers, known as "Hoodies" and this is why: Hooded mergansers are bold and kind of dumb. They are a diving bird and when they are underwater, you can get extremely close to them, increasing your success at jump shooting them when on the marsh. But you need to keep in mind that there are other diving birds that show the same characteristics but are not on the list of birds you can legally shoot, like grebes and loons. If you are playing "Red Light, Green Light" with a Hoodie, just make sure you positively identify that bird before you "water swat" it, that is shooting a bird on the water, not in flight. Water swatting is not illegal, just not very ethical or safe; but it is very easy. My dad always said, "As long as one toe is out of the water, it's fair game." Hoodies are very fun to shoot because of their speed, and they typically fly over water. When shooting at a Hoody on a creek you can usually see your shot pattern in the water, and it is a great way to practice leading shots and distances because you can see where your shot placement is hitting. Eating a Hoody ... not the most recommended bird. There was actually a period of time before I got Mark that I wouldn't even shoot them. A merganser's diet consists of mostly fish, therefore they taste like fish. Only fish should taste like fish, not birds. But they are great for dog retrieves and dog food; that way they still get used. Red-breasted mergansers are another common bird to find on the marsh. They are a little bigger than a Hoody. The drakes look kind of dirty with a bad hair day. Bright orange / reddish bill with teeth; all mergansers have a narrow-toothed bill. The common merganser, sometimes called "darts," are actually pretty big; they are found in large rivers with deeper water surrounded by Sea ducks.

BUFFLEHEAD

Another small diving duck that hunters get confused is the Bufflehead. Sometimes they are confused with the Hoody. They are roughly the same size and the drake heads both display bright white feathers. The legal difference between the Hoody and Bufflehead is that Mergansers have a separate daily bag limit. The Merganser season is the same as ducks, but you are allowed to harvest five Mergansers on top of your six ducks in your daily bag limit. Again, very important to positively identify waterfowl. Buffleheads have a common "duck-like" bill, whereas a merganser has a narrow "toothed" bill.

GOLDENEYE

On the Merrimack River seaward of the Rocks Village Bridge, you can almost always find Goldeneye; these are a medium size diving duck that whistle when they are in flight. I do not have much experience shooting these birds but if you have the proper setup, they are easy to decoy. I once jump shot a hen Goldeneye out on the marsh in Salisbury. There are two different types of Goldeneyes, the Common Goldeneye and the Barrow's Goldeneye. Both are legal to shoot but the Barrow's is very uncommon. Both Goldeneye look very similar, except the two drake species have a different white shape below their eyes. The Greater Scaup and Lesser Scaup; I have only ever seen these while bird watching in the off season. Hunters in this area do hunt them, but I have no experience in targeting them.

SEA DUCKS

There is a totally different category of ducks known as "Sea Ducks." They used to have a completely different season and bag limit from traditional "ducks" but that has now changed. Sea Ducks are made up of five species of diving ducks. These diving ducks are different than your typical Bufflehead or Goldeneye. These Sea Ducks live their entire lives at sea, some are native birds, but most come south from Canada and winter off of New England. Knowing your Sea Duck identification is extremely important because there is one Sea Duck that is prohibited to hunt: the **Harlequin Duck**. Study it, don't shoot it!

There are three types of **Scoters** that can be hunted. The White-winged Scoter, Black Scoter, and Surf Scoter. All three look fairly similar except the Surf Scoter has an extremely bright orange-colored bill that can been seen from a distance.

The next Sea Duck is the **Common Eider**. These birds are native to the area of the Great Marsh and spend the entire year breeding, raising young, and feeding in the open waters just outside the Great Marsh. During the summer season you can go to Gloucester Harbor and watch young Eiders learning how to dive and hunt for food. The Eider hens sometimes have up to twenty chicks swimming behind them. Sometimes there will be two or three hens to a large group of chicks teaching them how to forage for small fish and mollusks. When I was a kid, I never remembered seeing Eiders year-round, I just noticed it as I got older. I think the fact that Eiders that reside here year-round is fairly new, but I could be completely wrong. There is one more Sea Duck called a **Longtail**. For years they were referred to as "Oldsquaw," but that term is now offensive. The Longtail duck is a smaller Sea Duck and can be found all over the place. They live in the open ocean but you can get a chance at shooting one from shore depending on the marsh you are hunting. The drakes are absolutely beautiful and make a great standing mount.

These five Sea Ducks are sought out by hunters from all over the world. If you want to directly target Sea Ducks only, the cost is going to be substantial compared to outfitting yourself for jump shooting. You need at least an eighteen-foot boat with high gunwales and a reliable engine. These ducks are most commonly found in open ocean. They are kind of dumb and almost always decoy into a proper spread. But being on the open ocean in December and January off the coast of Massachusetts is not a smart move if you are not well equipped for this type of hunting. Just the boat alone is going to cost you at least $20,000 plus registration and insurance, dozens of decoys, and multiple trips to figure out how to do it. It would probably be much easier to just hire a guide to show you how it is done. There are two well-known Sea Duck guides in the area of the Great Marsh and they will show you how it is supposed to be done. Also, Sea Ducks taste like shit, so what's the point of shooting them if you are not going to eat them? I have shot a few Sea Ducks in my time but I do not specifically target them. There are actually a few places within the Great Marsh that you can shoot an Eider from shore, like at the end of Wingarsheek Beach in Gloucester. I have successfully shot a hen Eider from the edge of the marsh and had my dog retrieve it for me. Don't plan on shooting Eiders here without a retrieval method, the Annisquam River is far too deep and fast to walk out and retrieve a bird like you could in a low tide creek in the marsh. There is one more very unique Eider, known as the King Eider which has been shot in this area, but it is very uncommon. These birds are normally found and targeted by hunters in Alaska. I have seen two King Eiders off of Cape Ann before and guess where they were? Yes, singly hanging out in the middle of dozens of Harlequins off of Andrews Point. Don't even bother trying to target them, the chances of shooting a prohibited duck are very high; also, the chances of dying are up there too. They feed in the surf zone which is about fifty feet off of the rocks and 250' from houses, so you can't legally shoot there anyway. If you want to risk it all for a King Eider, just go to Alaska!

BRANT

Brant, Brant, Brant ... They are practically geese but super stupid. They show up late in the year and can be found feeding in the tide line on protected beaches. They usually show up in January and you can almost always find them at West Beach in Beverly Farms, but not to hunt. Just to watch. There are always a few hunters that show up targeting Brant just for the Waterfowl Challenge. The American Waterfowl Challenge is a list of forty-one targeted waterfowl species. Duck hunters travel around North America trying to complete the challenge. Massachusetts has about twenty of the forty-one species.

THE CANADA GOOSE

I think I have made my point throughout this book about these birds.

WHITE-FRONTED GOOSE

I have only seen a pair of these birds within the area of the Great Marsh, and it was a few years ago. A pair showed up on the Tendercrop Property off of Red Gate Road in Rowley. They stayed in the same field for almost a week and then I never saw them again. It was late goose season and I wouldn't be surprised if some poacher shot them from the road just for a sweet Instagram picture.

SNOW GEESE

They are very uncommon in this area, but there have been a small group that visit the Ipswich marsh around the week of Christmas. My dad sees them almost every year. These geese clearly know what they are doing or else they would be shot down. I have seen them once during this time over the years, but could never get a shot because they are about 1000 yards up. Just remember, Game Wardens know the difference between a Snow Goose and a Swan. Don't be stupid!

9

PUBLIC SPOTS

JUST IN THE NORTH SHORE ALONE THERE ARE at least twenty public duck hunting spots within a thirty-minute drive of each other. As I mentioned in the beginning, there's a law that protects you if you are lawfully engaged in Fowling, Fishing, or Navigating. This law gives you thousands of acres of huntable property. Now, that being said, you may know you are allowed to hunt there, but the general public may have no idea. Hunting is a privilege, not a right; there are far more anti-hunters and non-hunters than there are hunters. So, when one of these people see a person in camo with a gun, they will first think that you are a shooter instead of a hunter. When they call the police, they will report, "There's a man in dark clothing with a gun and they keep shooting!" The police only have one way to respond to this and that is multiple police officers responding to an active shooter. There is one very simple way to avoid that, depending on the town that you are hunting in that day; give that town's police department a call and let them know you will be hunting and where. This way, when someone calls the cops on you, the police will already know you are there. They still may send someone to check your license to carry, but they won't be coming in hot. Also, if you are on private property with written permission and the police arrive at your spot, do not approach them with a bad attitude; be polite and professional toward them. If you put your written permission in their face and say, "I HAVE PERMISSION TO BE HERE, I CALLED THE DEPARTMENT, I'M NOT DOING ANYTHING WRONG!" all that will do is make a bad name for yourself. That police officer who responds may have not gotten the memo that you did in fact make a courtesy call to the police department prior to your hunt. Another courtesy as a hunter is to not confront anyone who is acting negatively toward you. Just think of how that call is going to come in. "There's a man in the woods with a gun and he was being aggressive toward me and he pointed his gun at me!" There is no point trying to convince an anti-gun / hunter that you are lawfully allowed to be engaged in hunting in that area. A simple "Hello" or "Good morning" to any dog walker / hiker will let them know you are friendly and approachable. If the conversation goes south, just walk away without an exchange of words. If the interaction goes real south and you know you have not broken any laws and this anti-fun person is harassing you, call the Environmental Police. The Environmental Police will educate the harasser and let you go on your way before it becomes an "assault with a firearm" charge. Hunter Harassment is a criminal offense in Massachusetts; but can only be charged if the hunter who is being harassed is 100% legal.

The following areas are a few public places in Massachusetts you can find parking and walk in to go jump shooting:

Gloucester

- Sudbays
- Stone Pier
- Wingarsheek
- Goose Cove
- Lilly Pond

Ipswich

- Town Farm Road

Rowley

- Stackyard Road, Area A, B, C, D
- Sandy Point

Salisbury

- Salisbury Beach State Res.

Newbury

- Martin Burns WMA
- Crane Pond WMA
- William Forward WMA

10

TOP 5 RECIPES

YOU MAY HAVE NOTICED BY THIS POINT THAT MY dad is very old-school when it comes to duck hunting style, techniques, and stubbornness that have set him up for terrible duck recipes. His go-to duck and goose recipe, actually his only waterfowl recipe, is as follows: breast the duck / goose, no skin, and soak in a bowl of milk overnight. The next morning, toss in a frying pan and burn the hell out of it and serve with eggs, add copious amounts of salt and pepper. That was how I ate waterfowl for almost ten years. Now, as we have progressed in time and YouTube has made everyone's life much easier, you can look up anything, especially delicious waterfowl recipes that are incredible! There are thousands of different recipes to prepare these birds, and I am going to include a few of my favorites below.

Once you start shooting a ton of ducks and geese you will start to figure out what works best for you.

Skin-on Breasted Duck

DEPENDING ON THE TIME OF YEAR, YOU WILL find different levels of fat content below the skin of most ducks. During the early duck season when the water and air temperatures are still warm, ducks have just started building up the fat layer below their skin for the long cold winter months ahead. During the October duck season when I am primarily targeting flooded timber species like Green-winged Teal and Woodies or a good acorn fed Mallard, I may not clean these birds with the skin on. Their skin is so thin at this point, and it will probably be destroyed by the #4 shot blowing through their chest area anyway. If the current temperatures are between thirty and forty degrees, I will typically hang my birds on my barn by the head for a few days before processing them. This method allows the blood to drain from the meat and remove most of the "game taste." For Woodies and Teal, I will usually breast them out, and remove their wings and legs. If you have enough ducks at the end of the day, try to find the heart and collect a few of those; duck heart is very delicious, just super small so just toss them on the frying pan with some good olive oil or butter and some salt and pepper; you'll thank me later. But back to the flooded timber species; Teal and Woodies are very small ducks so you may need a few of them to make a meal. When these birds are breasted out you will have two small duck breasts. I will typically marinade them in a Worcestershire sauce / maple syrup marinade for a few days. This is a flavor combination that I like; you may not, it's okay, you do not have to agree with everything I say. After a few days in the fridge, I take them out, dry them off, and add a dry rub of spices that I would think will make it taste good. I usually stick to the same ingredients: salt, black pepper, red pepper flakes, onion powder, garlic powder, onion salt, thyme, coriander, dill, and pretty much anything that passes the sniff test before mixing them all in the same bowl. I specifically didn't mention any exact measurements and that is because I have absolutely no idea how much of each I add to the bowl. I have not made a bad spice mix yet. Once you find that perfect spice mixture, you'll know when your spouse sees you attempting to create a magic spice potion and the counter tops are absolutely covered in spices and they say, "Are you serious?" or "Do you have any idea what you're doing?" Your response should be, "Yes, I know exactly what I am doing!" Stop right there, that's usually when it is perfect. Depending on the time of day or when I plan to cook it, I may put this breasted spice-covered delectably pungent masterpiece back in the fridge for a day or two. Once it's time to cook, I go for the cast iron pan with an olive oil with a high smoke yield or butter. Get the pan real hot and toss the breasts on. Again, I am no chef, but I have sort of figured this part out. I like to have a pink center, I have no idea what temperature I achieve that at, but when I think it's time after a few minutes, I just cut into the thickest part and take a look. When it's ready, remove from the pan and serve with any vegetable you may pair with a good steak. This recipe works with all duck species you are willing to cook.

Bacon Wrapped Jalapeno Poppers

THESE ARE SO DAMN GOOD! I USUALLY DO A batch about once a year. This is a great way to make a few ducks go a long way. I typically use this method early season when I get a few Woodies and Teal. I start by breasting them out and placing in my traditional soy / Worcestershire / maple syrup marinade. This makes the meat taste very sweet. After soaking in the marinade for a few days, I remove and dry, then I cut the breasts into two- to three-inch-long strips. Go to the store and grab a tub of cream cheese, a pack of bacon, and a dozen full green Jalapeno peppers. Cut the Jalapenos in half from top to bottom and remove the seeds. I usually don't have the patience to remove all of the seeds so at some point someone is going to get an extremely spicy one. Its like Duck Popper Roulette when serving to a crowd. Somebody always asks, "Are these spicy?" I'll say, "They shouldn't be!" but only I know there are some seeds in at least one of them. You'll know when that person gets a seed. Hopefully they don't have ulcers! Anyway, back to cooking them. Once the peppers are hollowed out, fill them with cream cheese, place a duck strip on top, wrap with bacon, and secure it with a toothpick. Place these bacon-wrapped beauties on a cookie sheet, on top of foil, and toss in the oven. I always have to look up the basics like time and temperature. Usually 350 degrees for ten to fifteen minutes; maybe; just consult with Google. This will be a good time to cook the wings and legs too. Just watch them because they a very small and may cook quicker than the poppers.

Chicken of the Woods / Hen of the Woods Garlic Cream Sauce over Noodles with Teal

THIS RECIPE I JUST DISCOVERED THIS PAST season and God Damnit, it is fucking phenomenal! This past season was a very wet summer / fall which is great for mushroom hunting. I have recently gotten into mushroom hunting / mycology and the woods that surround the Great Marsh area have quite a few very delicious edible mushrooms.

It took me a few years of mushroom hunting to have enough confidence to look for other mushrooms besides the amazing Chicken of the Woods. This mushroom is bright orange, almost the same color as "Hunter Orange" and it sticks out like a sore thumb. It also primarily grows on dead oak trees, so proper tree identification is important too. Chicken of the Woods or COW can be sauteed in butter or oil; make sure you take a test bite and sit for a few minutes to make sure your body is okay with digesting wild mushrooms. These mushrooms pair great with any wild duck recipe, but my favorite combination is Wood Duck, Teal, or Mallard, breasted with the skin on, seared in a Hen of the Woods garlic cream sauce. I'll try to help you get to this point.

I think I have covered how to get a duck, but when you are duck hunting in flooded timber before you get to the marsh during the cold season, you will be walking through oak forests to get to good flooded timber hunting spots.

The Hen of the Woods grow at the base of Oak trees after a wet, rainy summer. The fruiting body is found primarily in late October right around when hunting season starts. Keep in mind that Hen of the Woods usually come back in the same spot year after year if you properly harvest them.

I'm not going to be responsible for edible mushroom hunting identification, I'll leave that up to you so you can't hold me accountable for misidentifying a mushroom and having violent diarrhea for days. That has never happened to me because I have been extremely cautious when studying the identification of edible mushrooms. So, in a perfect world, you now have a dead Wood duck in your bag limit and on your way out of the woods you have found a one-pound Hen of the Woods. During the early duck season, I almost always have duck marinading in my fridge, so if I find a mushroom, I can almost always prepare it with some sort of duck meat. You'll need to thoroughly wash the Hen of the Woods with cold water to remove the insects and dirt. If you're lucky, you'll miss a small slug and get to pan fry and consume it later. I like to slice and chop up the mushroom into two-to-three-inch pieces and sauté in oil until I know that they are fully cooked. Once I know they are cooked, I'll add some chicken broth and heavy cream and all sorts of onion / garlic spices. I usually use whatever type of noodles that are in the pantry; cook them separately. Cook your duck breast separately also. Once your noodles and duck are cooked the way you want them, put the noodles on your plate, then duck breast, then pour the mushroom garlic cream sauce over everything and serve. You can thank me later with this one too; this recipe will blow you away.

Chicken of the Woods

Hen of the Woods

Seared duck breast with Hen of the Woods risotto and noodles.

Goose Pastrami

MOST PEOPLE ABSOLUTELY HATE THE TASTE OF goose, resulting in the lack of interest in targeting them in the first place. About three years ago I discovered an incredible goose pastrami recipe, and it has changed the way I consume geese. It is extremely time consuming, but totally worth it and when you shoot forty geese during early season, you're going to want to know this recipe. Just cleaning forty geese will take you about an hour. My friend James taught me a very efficient way to breast out a full goose in a timely manner. Just above the breast bone toward the neck you will feel the wind pipe of the goose. Slice an opening by cutting through the feathers, skin, and windpipe, insert your fingers into this cavity and peel the skin back toward the feet, exposing the breast meat. Instead of plucking feathers and cutting back the skin, which when you first start may take ten to twenty minutes per bird, the breast meat will be exposed and be ready to be cut out. Now that you have cut out eighty breasts and have about fifty pounds of bird meat, you're going to ask yourself, "WTF do I do with all of this?" Make sure you have two clean five-gallon buckets with lids. I will put forty breasts in each bucket and add cold water, brown sugar, soy sauce, and a few spices. Luckily, I have a game fridge that I can put these buckets in to soak the meat for three to five days. I wouldn't recommend soaking the meat in buckets not in a fridge; during early goose season the temperature outside is still between fifty to eighty degrees, not a good temperature for meat. This recipe will also work with a pair of goose breasts during the normal season, you just need to scale it way down from the bucket method. So, now that you have your marinaded goose meat, the next step is to cure the meat. For this step you will need a few more ingredients, most importantly curing salt. I always use Morton's Tender Quick Curing Salt. I usually pick up a few pounds of it prior to the hunting season. Now, I have no idea what Tender Quick does exactly to the meat, but if you cure it correctly, the meat is outstanding. I believe it pulls the moisture out of the meat or something like that. But during this curing stage you will want to create another all-spice mixture including the Tender Quick. You want every piece of bird meat covered with this all-spice meat magic. Depending on the scale of meat you are trying to cure, you can put the meat into freezer bags, remove the air, and put into the fridge. Every day flip the bags so that the meat cures properly. After three to five days, remove from the fridge and rinse off all of the breasts. You should notice that the meat is kind of firm feeling. Soak all the breasts in cold water for at least thirty to sixty minutes prior to going to the last step. You want to remove all of the curing salt; this step is very important; Tender Quick is not for human consumption; it can make you very sick. The cold-water soak removes the Tender Quick. Now that you have your meat prepared and it has been almost a week to ten days since you shot them, it is now finally time for the smoker (or grill if you don't have a smoker yet). This step is to create the best flavor combination of an all-spice meat magic flavor bomb that when you smoke it for an hour, it should give you full body chills when you bite into it. I'll include a spice list following this that you can choose from to make your own meat magic flavor. Once your meat has a flavorful spice rub, it's now time to put in the smoker. Depending on the type of smoker you may have the option to add wood chips for a smoky flavor. I usually smoke the meat for about an hour, using a meat thermometer. I make sure the internal temperature is at least 155–165 degrees before removing and preparing to serve. This pastrami can be eaten hot, cold, or reheated. I vacuum seal and freeze the rest of the pastrami. The absolute best lunch recipe is to thinly slice the pastrami, pan fry it in butter, and make a sandwich with some fancy mustard. Absolutely incredible. You can thank Kagan for introducing that method to me.

Skin-on goose pastrami.

No skin goose pastrami.

Skin-on duck pastrami.

MEAT MAGIC SPICE LIST:

- Salt
- Course sea salt
- Brown sugar
- Black pepper
- Red pepper flakes
- Onion powder / salt
- Garlic powder / salt
- Dill
- Thyme
- Coriander
- Paprika

These are usually my go to meat magic spices.

CYNDY GRAY'S BAKED STRIPER

THIS RECIPE IS FAIRLY SIMPLE; MY MOM ALWAYS used the same white ceramic baking dish every time she cooked striper. She would take one to two filets and place them in the bottom of the pan. I would recommend using butter or olive oil on the bottom of the pan so it doesn't get stuck. Pre-heat the oven to 425 degrees and prep the fish. First get one to two sleeves of Ritz Crackers and smash them up inside the plastic sleeves. Spread the crumbled crackers over the top of the fish and pour melted butter over the top. You can either squeeze lemon juice on it now or after it is cooked, or both, it's going to be delicious regardless. Bake for ten to twelve minutes or until it becomes easy to pull apart with a fork. Serve with baked potato or green beans.

Cyndy Gray's Famous Fried Lobster

LOBSTERS MUST BE COOKED ALIVE, SO YOU HAVE to cook them within a day or two from being caught. They will stay alive in the fridge for a day or two, but the sooner they get into a pot the better. I was always taught to boil a pot of water and once boiling, place the lobsters into the boiling water and watch for the water to return to a boil. Once boiling, set a ten-minute timer and remove. They will come out perfect every time. When planning to deep fry some lobster, you will use this same process but remove the lobsters eight minutes after the boil. That way when they cook in the deep fryer, they do not become over cooked in the oil. Get yourself a few packs of New England Batter. Make a dry and wet batter. For the wet batter, I usually just mix it with water until all the batter mixes with the water. I always just eyeball the mixes so I really have no idea what the exact measurements are. After cleaning the lobster meat from the shells, you will want to place the meat in the wet batter to cover all sides of the meat, then directly into the dry batter covering all sides also. Do this same method for eight to ten pieces. You will want to pick up a deep fryer prior to this. This method works in a frying pan, but trust me, after tasting this, you'll want to invest in a tabletop deep fryer to make this process a little easier. Place the fryer on 350 degrees, wait until the oil reaches that temperature and lower the battered meat into the oil. This doesn't take long, just make sure you are watching the color of the batter. Once the batter turns a deep golden color, they are ready to remove from the oil. WAIT FOR THEM TO COOL! Wait for these beauties to cool before putting a 350-degree oiled lobster chunk into your mouth. Trust me, it's worth the wait. Melt down a stick or two of butter and hammer it with some salt and maybe a squeeze of a lemon. You will never want lobster any other way for the rest of your life, I promise!

11

JUMP SHOOTING STORIES

I HAD DISCOVERED LATE IN THE SEASON A Mallard honey hole at Bartletts Farm. A hay field had flooded and created a perfect late season open water duck habitat. I had jumped this hole about three or four times in a seven-day period and was batting 100. I was super focused, and you could use an overgrown trail to get within thirty feet of these feeding birds without them knowing you were there. I went in there with Mark one morning and spotted about thirty beautiful late season Greenheads feeding in the shallow flooded field. The open water was only about a twenty feet by twenty feet hole and was packed with birds. I slowly snuck up to these birds, telling myself, "Don't flock shoot, don't flock shoot, don't flock shoot." I convinced myself not to flock shoot, then I told myself, "Pick one Greenhead, pick one Greenhead, pick one Greenhead." Okay, got it! Don't flock shoot and pick one Greenhead. Once I was confident in that series of events, I started to think about how I was going to cook not one but two Greenheads after I made two perfect shots. These were late season freshwater-fed Mallards and I knew they were going to have a thick layer of fat and would make for a delicious maple and soy marinaded, pan fried meal, I could taste it. Now with hope of a good meal in my future, I was slowly getting to the tree that I have successfully shot from in the recent past. I saw the Greenhead I wanted, raised my over under with my first shot coming from the improved choke, a deadly option inside of thirty feet. I aimed at the Mallard as three dozen birds blast in every direction; I slap the trigger and BANG! Nothing falls. Confused at what just happened, I lock on to another Greenhead that is now at thirty yards, BANG! Nothing falls. Now frantically looking around to see where the birds are, I reload, look around, and the birds are 100 yards away. Mark is bullshit that I missed, I'm bullshit that I missed, and I stood there in absolute defeat wondering how the hell I missed a perfectly good shot. As I walked back to my truck, I replayed the situation and realized I got distracted by the meal before I even had the chance to cook it. This is a unique situation but it could vary in different ways for you when hunting. You must be extremely focused on the target to deliver a good effective shot to get birds on the ground. The lesson here is to remain focused while jump shooting, especially when you know where the birds are and they don't know where you are. There are many steps you need to take to be able to get you in a good spot to take a good shot. One wrong move and you'll screw it all up. Which is going to happen if you are a new hunter or have been doing it for fifty years. Mistakes will happen.

First Day at Kagan's

THE FIRST DAY HUNTING AT KAGAN'S NEW HOUSE will forever be burned into my memory. It was many years ago but the day he closed on the house we went out back for a jump shoot. We refer to the back of his property as "Out Back" because behind his property is a few hundred acre secluded piece of the Great Marsh surrounded by private properties, and there is no public access to it. The marsh "Out Back" has three giant salt pannes and miles of creeks that we will later in life master the jump shoot of every square foot of this marsh. Kagan got a stupid good deal on this house; I'm not going to mention figures, but it could never happen again. The previous owner was still living in the house, but I wasn't there to see the house, I was there for the access to this secluded marsh. We went to the first salt panne known as "The Panne" and set up layout blinds and a shitload of decoys. I brought my camera with me and we waited.

I don't know the number of birds we shot and it doesn't even matter. I got the best picture of Kagan that will go down in history of absolute pure obsession and love. By the purchasing of that property, Kagan's life has changed for the better in every way possible. He can now walk out his back door and duck hunt; there are very few waterfowl hunters that will ever have that opportunity to do so.

First day at Kagan's shooting geese on "the big panne."

PETE BOWMAN

ONE OF MY DAD'S FAVORITE HUNTING STORIES happened back in 2005, give or take a year. Every Friday night my late best friend, Peter Bowman, would sleep over and we would go jump shooting in Gloucester the following morning with my dad and the two dogs. My dad's hunting dogs were Smokey, the chocolate Lab, and White Sox, a black Golden Retriever. White Sox "Whitey" never got a bird, but she went hunting every single time for almost fourteen years; she made it to sixteen. Whitey's mother, a purebred Golden Retriever got knocked up in my backyard by the town mutt before the stupid leash laws became a thing. Smokey was a savage hunter; she got me her first bird at the age of four months and brought me in a goose at six months. She hated geese, but not in a bad way; she wasn't afraid of them but just wanted to kill them. Her drive for retrieving birds was like no other; she never listened and couldn't sit still, but when a bird dropped in the water, she would not quit until she got it.

It was an overcast low tide morning jump shoot at Stone Pier in Gloucester. We had parked at the pier and walked out toward the Annisquam River hoping to jump some Black Ducks along the way. We walked for an hour with no success. As we began to head back to the truck, I looked down the big creek and saw a handful of Hooded Mergansers diving. Pete and I played "Red Light, Green

Light" for about fifteen minutes to try to approach these Hoodies to get a good shot. Once I got close enough, approximately twenty yards, I shouldered my gun and shot the first bird that moved. Smokey bolted into the water. I could tell that the bird was crippled because it was still swimming upright but was dragging a wing. If you have a safe shot, shoot the bird again so that it dies and will be easier to retrieve. But Smokey was heading to the bird, so I couldn't take a shot because I would be shooting over the top of the dog and that is just a terrible idea. As the dog approached the crippled Hoody, the bird would dive under the water to try to get away. It would pop up thirty feet away and Smokey would charge after it and it would dive. Smokey chased this bird for almost ten minutes as we watched from the bank. Like I said before, she wouldn't listen or ever quit, so I couldn't call her away from the bird to place a safe shot. Eventually I got a shot on the bird, three or four, but at this time the bird was outside of fifty yards. Smokey was still chasing the bird, but I had no shells left and she wouldn't come in. Pete Bowman was not a hunter, but when he wanted something, he did whatever he could to get it. He noticed that Smokey was struggling with this retrieve, so he decided to give her some help. Pete was wearing a winter hat, black and grey drug rug, jeans, and boots that went up to his lower shins. This was December or January, water was about forty-something degrees, and there's Pete running toward Smokey in knee-deep water.

Once he got to the area of the creek where the bird was, he began pivoting side to side as he watched the Hoody swim side to side underwater. Smokey was now watching Pete chase the bird. Pete looks over his shoulder, pivots around forward as the Hoody swims right between his legs. He reaches down into the knee-deep water, grabs the Hoody by the neck and raises both arms in the air like he just scored a goal. I can still picture him walking back to shore, shit-eating grin from ear to ear, soaked from the waist down with Smokey by his side.

Six Goose Creek

GROWING UP WHILE JUMP SHOOTING THE MARSH off of Town Farm Rd. in Ipswich, we would see old hunting camps out on the marsh. My dad always told me, "If you ever get the chance to stay overnight in one of those, never deny the offer." Some of these camps have been erected for over a hundred years. This past season, I was invited to stay overnight at one of these duck camps. We planned the trip a week in advance and when the time came, a powerful Nor'easter was supposed to hit our direct location. I didn't call it off; this was something I had been looking forward to for twenty years. I packed out my canoe with way too much stuff and started dragging it to the closest creek, which was about 200 yards. I made it only seventy-five yards before I started shedding weight due to how difficult it was to drag. The essentials went first, fifty pounds of firewood. The beer and food stayed. Eventually I made it to the creek and at this point the rain had just started, but I was already smoked, calves were on fire, and I still had a quarter mile to go. I floated the canoe and started paddling, there was a decent amount of rain, and I was protected from the wind by the high banks of the creek. It was very peaceful as I paddled through the creeks, the Nova laying on the rest ready to go if I had the opportunity to jump a duck as I rounded each corner, getting closer to camp. I didn't think I would jump anything because Mark was swimming next to me as we navigated the narrow creeks, but it didn't matter. I was in my favorite place on this planet, doing my favorite activity, with my best bud Mark, paddling my way to a camp that I've spent my life dreaming about. Eventually, I ran out of water and had to put my canoe back up top and begin dragging again. Now the canoe had two inches of rainwater in it; adding to the overall weight. At this point in time, I was still annihilated from the first 100 yards. But now I only have 200 yards to go. In between these 200 yards were two large salt pannes. The water in the pannes were not deep enough for me to sit in the canoe to paddle across so I walked the edges of the panne and dragged the canoe behind me. There was the camp now only fifty yards from me, no windows, only one door. But there it was, this camp has been creating lifelong memories for over a hundred years. I am not the first and will not be the last who has made the journey out from Town Farm Road. What I didn't realize when I got this close was there was another creek between me and the camp. I dragged the canoe to that creek, offloaded all my gear and walked it to the camp. I left the canoe anchored to the creek bank for the guys who were heading out after they got out of work. I didn't even have a key to the camp, I was hoping that Jody wouldn't bail because of the weather conditions and leave me stranded. Now at camp, I didn't waste any daylight, I set dozens of Divebomb silos and a few floaters and finally took a seat. There were plenty of birds flying in the background, but nothing looking at what I had to offer. But again, I did not care. Shooting light came to an end and Jody eventually made his way out with the key. We opened camp and started a fire. As the sun set, the wind began to pick up and the tide began to rise. As we attempted to dry our rain-soaked clothing, the wind started to really crank. The high tide that evening was around eight p.m. and the marsh was flooded at six p.m. This told me that the wind coming from the Northeast was creating a massive storm surge directly affecting the tide. The tide just kept coming in, Jody and I were completely stranded at camp, the entire marsh now looked like open ocean, and the wind was punishing the roof of the camp. The structure of the camp was built on top of pilings and was about three feet above the marsh. Inside we were warm, but we were looking at the water line on the inside of camp. With the spring full moon tides, the camp fully floods out. We were hoping that did not happen to us. Beat up from the trek out to camp we had an early bedtime.

We woke up early in the morning; Kagan, Nate, and son Josh were heading out to our location in the pitch black, fully flooded marsh and rain / snow mixture going sideways at forty-five mph. There honestly could not be a worse time to navigate the marsh, but if I trusted anyone to do it in these conditions, it would be these three people. They didn't fall into any holes, creeks, pannes, or any dangerous part of the marsh. They made it to the location of the canoe, one by one entered the canoe, and pushed across the creek to get to the other side. I was shocked that the canoe was still in the same place after the huge tides and powerful winds overnight. They made it to camp, we went inside, cooked up some pancakes, made some terrible coffee, and waited for the sun to rise. We first set up on the backside of the camp to attempt to block the wind. I have noticed in some cases that birds typically do not like to fly directly over objects on the marsh. In this case, birds were not flying very close to the camp, but we did not have any other options. As the tide receded, we split up and went to some fixed blinds on the marsh a few hundred yards apart. Kagan and I went to the far blind, and Jody, Nate, and Josh set up a few decoys and waited for the birds in the close blind. Kagan, Mark, and I staged up in an old three-man blind and waited for some pass shooting opportunities. It wasn't long before a beautiful drake Red-headed Merganser flew behind our blind and landed about seventy yards away. Kagan kept his eye on him as he swam in the creek. The bird started swimming toward our location and eventually got up to fly. Kagan raised his gun, gave the bird a ten-inch lead, pulled the trigger, and followed through with his lead. This bird folded up and landed on the other side of the creek. It was not quite dead, so Kagan took its head off with a follow-up shot before it had the chance to dive and get away from the dog. The bird's final resting place was now two creeks away from us. It was now Mark's turn. Mark knew there was a bird down, but he could not find it. I let him work for a few minutes, attempting to yell and point in the direction of the bird, but he is not trained to know what the hell I was talking about. So, I bent over and ripped up a hand full of marsh mud, balled it up and lobbed it across the two creeks near the dead bird. Mark was on the other side of the creek; he watched the ball leave my arm and land next to the Merganser. Once he put eyes on the bird he sprinted to action. This was Kagan's first time hunting over Mark. As Marcus grabbed that bird, crossed one creek, then another, Kagan and I were so proud him. Kagan and I have done some crazy retrieves of birds and every single time after hours of trying to retrieve a single bird we always say, "Jesus Christ, we need a duck dog!" This was the first time in seven years that we didn't have to say it. Shooting a Merganser isn't something that we would normally do, they smell and taste like shit, but it was one of those shots that we couldn't let it fly away. Now with the dog, it's justifiable to shoot any legal bird regardless of what they taste like. With one bird in the bag, an amazing retrieve from Mark, we started to pack up and make our way back to Town Farm Road.

TO MOST HUMANS, WHETHER THEY KNOW IT OR not, hunting is a natural instinct, but it is soon to be forgotten if we do not continue to pass on what we know to the next generation. I am not writing this to take my chance at fame. I am writing this book to be remembered, to document my experience and life stories. I am by no means an expert at duck hunting, but I feel like I am damn good at it. There are plenty of people who are better at it than I am and many who are just starting to figure it out. I hope this reaches the correct people and they can learn something to make them a better hunter and most importantly, pass along to someone else what they have learned.

www.ingramcontent.com/pod-product-compliance
Lightning Source LLC
Chambersburg PA
CBHW060434130626
46555CB00005B/2357